STORY $ELLING

HOLLYWOOD SECRETS REVEALED

HOW TO SELL
Without Selling

By Telling Your Brand Story

Published by CelebrityPress®, Orlando, FL

CelebrityPress® is a registered trademark

Printed in the United States of America.

ISBN: 978-0-9886418-7-7
LCCN: 2013937895

This publication is designed to provide accurate and authoritative information with regard to the subject matter covered. It is sold with the understanding that the publisher is not engaged in rendering legal, accounting, or other professional advice. If legal advice or other expert assistance is required, the services of a competent professional should be sought. The opinions expressed by the authors in this book are not endorsed by CelebrityPress® and are the sole responsibility of the author rendering the opinion.

Most CelebrityPress® titles are available at special quantity discounts for bulk purchases for sales promotions, premiums, fundraising, and educational use. Special versions or book excerpts can also be created to fit specific needs.

For more information, please write:

CelebrityPress®
520 N. Orlando Ave, #2
Winter Park, FL 32789
or call 1.877.261.4930

Visit us online at www.CelebrityPressPublishing.com

HOLLYWOOD SECRETS REVEALED

HOW TO SELL
Without Selling

By Telling Your Brand Story

By
Nick Nanton Esq.
and
J.W. Dicks Esq.

CELEBRITY PRESS®
Winter Park, Florida

CONTENTS

ACT I
THE POWER OF STORYSELLING™
HOW IT WORKS

CHAPTER 1
STORYSELLING™
In The Beginning

CHAPTER 2
THE SCIENCE OF STORYSELLING™
Hitting the "Love Hormone"

CHAPTER 3
STORYSELLING™ IS BELIEVING:
The Truth About Fact and Fiction

ACT II
THE BUSINESS OF STORYSELLING™
HOW IT WORKS

<u>ACT III</u>
STORYSELLING™ IN ACTION
REALIZING RESULTS

FOREWORD

StorySelling™ is such a cool word.

I wish I'd thought of it. Trademarked it.

It gripes me that Nanton and Dicks now "own" it, and I do not.

Every life is a story. Every person has been immersed in story, being told stories, being sold to with stories, and telling stories, their entire lives. The 'human interest story' made the magazine industry; now it has filled the TV airwaves with "reality shows" and their true-life stories of pawnshop owners and tow truck operators and alligator farmers and tattoo artists. Advertising has been dominated by 'slice of life' stories and by testimonials (1st-person stories) for my entire life, at least tripled. Anyone pronouncing this approach to advertising obsolete is blind, deaf and *definitely* dumb.

The fact is: stories are more *persuasive* than facts or logic, information or education, even personal observation. All religions have been and are sold by story. Hordes of 30, 40, even 50 year old women who never before thought once of going to an adult boutique (sex shop) in search of furry handcuffs and riding crops were driven there by a fictional story, *Fifty Shades of Gray*. Each person who has campaigned successfully for the U.S. presidency has brought forward a compelling and inspiring personal narrative. Disney World is a marketing and moneymaking marvel greater than any other, because it immerses its guests into one story after another.

Facts are instantly suspect. Doubted. Challenged. Everyone knows statistics lie. A picture is no longer worth 1,000 words, because we all know how easily they are doctored, photo-shopped. But a compelling story fascinates. It circumvents skepticism shields. It makes people feel. Imagine. Identify with. Want to know more.

More people know fiction than fact. Fewer than 10% of Americans can name a single Supreme Court Justice, but everybody knows Robin Hood and *the story of* Robin Hood. Mickey Mouse is the most recognized 'person' in the world. Most investors know "*the story of* Warren Buffet" as he has gone to great pains to promulgate – but I have studied the facts of Buffet, and can usually surprise investors who think they know about Buffett with three statements of fact. Ask people to name a detective. Nobody can name a real one. Everybody can name Sherlock Holmes. Huge numbers of people send letters every year to Sherlock Holmes in London, England, asking for his help with everything from a lost, beloved pet to a conviction that people around them are plotting their murder. I was at the Sherlock Holmes Museum in London, essentially a clever gift shop, and overheard one tourist telling another, "Well, this is interesting, but I was hoping we'd see where he really lives."

Against all this, in foolish opposition to all this, most businesspeople and salespeople still insist on focusing on products and services, features and benefits, facts and figures, and worst of all, price – then they wonder why they get commoditized, why customers are hard to interest then fickle and hard to keep.

This is the consistent failure of advertising and marketing.

The whole world – everyone's prospects – are climbing up onto laps and begging, *"Tell me a story."* NOT "sell me something." NOT "educate and inform me."

Pay attention to Campbell's Soup, one of the most enduring, valuable brands. Soup is a dull and boring product. Campbell's thrives by StorySelling™. Through the stories they show and tell of family life and good parenting and healthy, happy, appreciative kids, they are able to attach deep emotional meanings to a mundane commodity. And that is their only real equity. It's not in soup recipes. It's not in distribution – the soup aisle has other brands. Other soups at cheaper prices, too. And, of course, other soup does get sold. But over generations, no competitor has weakened Campbell's dominance – because no other soup company has so interwoven itself with the story of the American family. Thus, if you play "name the first thing that comes into your mind" with "soup", Campbell's is the only brand named. (A generic 'chicken soup' is said by most – because, by the way, there's a story attached to chicken soup. Campbell's is the 2nd most given response.)

If you think this doesn't apply to you, because your business is different, your customers are different, etc., you are dead wrong, and this fine book will hopefully convince you otherwise.

Although I never used the term 'StorySelling™', I have spent my entire life selling by story, for myself and clients, via every media, to every kind of customer – in TV infomercials; in long-form print ads aimed at sophisticated audiences (such as readers of Investor's Business Daily) and arguably unsophisticated audiences (such as readers of rural newspapers); in direct-mail, B2C and B2B; in selling items priced at $10 and at $100,000.00; in marketing the services of upscale financial advisors to affluent retirees, business programs to dentists, acne remedy to teens and their moms, expense reduction consulting to corporate CEO's, and moneymaking opportunities to blue-collar, blue-jeans workin' folk. I am a wealthy man because of the power of story, and as one of the highest paid direct response copywriters in the world, I make a lot of other people wealthy by telling their stories for them.

I can unequivocally assure you, these authors, Nick Nanton and Jack Dicks, are masters of the art, science and process

of identifying, crafting and presenting stories for strategic purposes – selling, fundraising, motivating, inspiring, changing minds, attracting followings. I know their work personally. I have brought them into client situations, elite mastermind meetings. Recommended them. Directly provided them with hundreds of thousands of dollars in business. Their book is rich with examples, authoritative research, direct 'case history' experience. It gives you practical blueprints, nearly templates. Most importantly, it proves its case beyond shadow of doubt: *you* should be StorySelling™.

I'll mention one important thing – there are many, but I'll mention one – to look for and gain from this book. It is one thing to identify your story that best represents you and to be able to tell it well. It is another, more significant thing to have your customers and others in your marketplace know that story so well they could tell it. It is yet another, even more significant thing to actually have your customers and others in your marketplace telling your story for you, about you, in introducing others to you. In other words, there are different levels of StorySelling™. This book can carry you through the first to the second, and through the second to the third.

I have only one severe criticism of this book. It's actually giving away too much of the store for the price of a book. They shouldn't have.

Dan S. Kennedy

Author, *No B.S. Trust-Based Marketing* and 18 other business books (www. NoBSBooks.com), marketing strategy consultant, direct-response copywriter, and editor, *No B.S. Marketing Letter* (www.DanKennedy.com)

PREFACE
JACOB'S TURN

You're sitting in an airport terminal, waiting for your next flight. You travel a lot, so layovers become a fact of life. To make matters worse, the terminal is crowded. Not a lot of space. That means when you sit down, you don't get to keep an empty seat between you and the next guy - nope, you have to sit right down next to him.

Not that it's that big a deal. He seems nice enough. In this particular case, he has his laptop open – and you happen to glance over at the screen. And you notice a picture of a boy, about four or five, in a baseball uniform. You smile and you can't help yourself. You turn to the guy and you say, "Cute kid."

Those two words end up transforming your life and your business.

It was April of 2009 at Midway Airport in Chicago; Nick was the one who happened to see the boy's photo. As mentioned, of the two of us, he travels the most and ends up spending more time in terminals than Tom Hanks did in that movie - you know, the movie where he *lived* in a terminal.

The guy with the laptop? His name turned out to be Jim Titus – and the picture on his display was of his four year-old son, Jacob Titus. His response to Nick's compliment was, "He's an amazing blessing to us." He also added that his son had Down Syndrome.

The conversation continued. Jim told Nick that he worked for UPS; Nick told Jim about our Celebrity Branding Agency and how we managed clients all across the country and helped them achieve high-profile status. He also mentioned his experience in entertainment, producing award-winning albums and television shows.

Jim may have lived in Indiana, as far away from the entertainment industry as you can imagine, but he was still very interested in Nick's background - for a very specific reason. Because of his son's condition, Jim's family was very involved with the Down Syndrome Support Association of Southern Indiana. The organization was going to hold a silent auction during its annual Buddy Walk event – and Jim wondered if Nick had any "celebrity items" he could contribute. Nick agreed to look into it and they exchanged email addresses. A few weeks later, Nick sent Jim a couple of CDs autographed by country music stars Rascal Flatts and Bucky Covington for the auction, and that was that.

Except it wasn't.

Four months later, Jim emailed Nick an article his wife had written about their son which was entitled, "Jacob's Turn." It was a beautifully written article about Jacob's experience playing T-ball that year (which is why Jacob was wearing the baseball uniform in the photo) and it moved both of us to tears. Here are a few excerpts from her story:

When I signed my kids up this year [for baseball,] I was unsure of how it would go. Not for my daughter Lauren, 10 or my older son Matthew, 8, but for my youngest. I didn't know how the coaches would feel about having him on their team. I wondered how the parents of the other children would react and then there were the kids. What I did know is that my kid loved to play ball and he would get his chance. My youngest son loves to bat, loves to run, loves to play catcher. Jacob also happens to have Down syndrome."

His coach's name was Eric Sprigler. The first time he met Jacob he smiled, shook his hand, and asked if he was ready to play some ball. Jacob assured him he was and so, just like that, it started. The team had two assistant coaches Brian Hooper and Kevin Reed. All three of these men were patient and kind. They seemed genuinely proud of what Jacob could do and how much he improved. As there should be in t-ball, there were lots of high fives and people saying "Good job!" and "Nice try!" There were also more smiles than I could ever count....

But still, how I worried and watched. Watched and worried. What were the other parents thinking? Were they saying he didn't belong? I didn't have to wonder for long... When Jacob was at bat he had an amazing cheering section. It seemed to include everyone watching the game. Jacob would make it to first, everyone would cheer and he would take a couple of bows. The first base coach told me he was saying, "Thank you, thank you" as he bowed. Several parents from our team and from other teams would take pictures of Jacob for us and send them to us.

As a parent, you put your children out there. You pray that people will be kind to them. You want them to accept them and you want them to belong. You sometimes dare to hope that someone might even notice what a great kid you have and appreciate him for who he is. It was a beautiful season. Jacob and his family were given a time we will always remember. It wasn't a time that was centered around doctor visits or therapies or special teachers. It was time for Jacob to just be a kid, like everyone else, swinging for the fence. His dad and I want to express our appreciation to the coaches, parents, players, umpires and the community. We live in such a great place and if "Baseball is life," then Jacob will be just fine.

Jacob's story was amazing – his skills developed over the season and his team almost won the championship; the season ended with the coaches giving Jacob a ball autographed by the local minor league baseball team, The Louisville Bats, as a special prize for his hard work and dedication.

We both felt Jacob's story was important – and we wondered how we could help the story go viral to somehow benefit the Down Syndrome Support Association. We finally brainstormed the perfect answer. That answer? Tell the story in *movie* form – a film that could be placed online and potentially reach millions of people.

Movies are, of course, an expensive proposition – but, luckily, we also had access to a circle of expert marketers and entrepreneurs who would probably be willing to help.

So, we created **Marketers for Good** (now known as **Entrepreneurs International Foundation**), a non-profit organization whose initial project would be the short film, "Jacob's Turn." With financial backing from all our new "executive producers," Nick flew into the Titus' home town of Floyds Knobs, Indiana in May of 2010 with a film crew – and, with the community's help, they recreated Jacob's magical first season playing on a baseball field.

Through interviews with Jacob's family, his coaches, his teammates and other townspeople – and some beautiful cinematography provided by our crew – Jacob's story was fully realized in a seven-minute short film that we posted online and that quickly did, in fact, go viral; it ended up spurring donations to help pay for some of Jacob's special therapies and classes, and to top it all off, the film was even honored with an Emmy award.

But none of this would have happened if it hadn't been such a strong and moving story to begin with. When viewers watched this film, they connected with Jacob and his family in such a deep emotional way that they frankly felt compelled to donate money.

Bringing to life this very personal story made such a huge difference that we were shocked. We already knew that stories made a big difference to "moving the needle" through our own personal experiences – but "Jacob's Turn" took things to a whole new level.

So we talked about *why* a story like this made such a difference. It led to more far-ranging discussions about how powerful narratives made a huge impact in other crucial sociological areas, such as religion. For example, what is the life of Jesus routinely called? "The Greatest Story Ever Told." Almost all faiths have a bedrock *personal* story that inspires its followers – the Mormons with Joseph Smith, Islam with Muhammad, Protestants with Martin Luther, even Buddhism with…well, Buddha.

Then there's politics, where a story can either sink or save a candidate. In 2012, Mitt Romney's perceived "story" as the rich out-of-touch guy definitely put a damper on his campaign at first. Barack Obama's "hope and change" narrative, in contrast, connected big time with voters in 2008, vaulting him in the primary race past the presumed front-runner, Hillary Clinton.

In both cases, and in almost all political races, whatever story sticks to a candidate usually determines his or her fate – more so than the facts or actual policy points. That point is reflected in a 2012 article posted on the Pew Research Center's website, Journalism.org, "The Master Character Narratives in Campaign 2012":

"…election reporting is heavily influenced by a handful of master narratives, or what some scholars have called "meta-narratives," about the candidates. While every campaign is an ongoing story, the theory argues that journalists' choice of facts and incidents is influenced by certain perceived character traits or themes about the candidates. And one concern about these master narratives is that they become self-perpetuating. Facts and anecdotes that illustrate ongoing storylines become magnified, critics worry, and events that do not fit with those running

storylines get overlooked."

In other words, a story is not necessarily created from the facts – more often, *facts are bent to fit the story.* This again reflects the incredible power of story-telling.

This, of course, prompted even more questions:

- Why were stories so effective in persuading people?
- Was there a reason fiction could actually triumph over fact?
- How could stories be put to work for our clients?
- What kinds of stories were most effective for businesses and entrepreneurs?
- How could those stories best be told?

The answers to those questions caused us to rethink our business models and, ultimately, to write this book. Frankly, we couldn't believe what our research uncovered. All of this information is, of course, available through various sources, but we wanted to bring it all together for the first time.

Read on to discover the secrets behind what we call "StorySelling™." We can pretty much guarantee a happy ending.

INTRODUCTION

A few years ago, we wrote the best-selling book, "Celebrity Branding You," which detailed the system we developed to help our clients become the "Go-To Experts" in their particular fields, through what we saw as a revolutionary series of steps that both established *credibility* and *visibility* in powerful and long-lasting ways.

Our personality-driven methodology proved to be more successful than we imagined. By creating our own online and offline media outlets, which included TV shows, newspapers, online content, magazines and books, we were able to guarantee our clients massive media exposure that they would have otherwise been unable to attain – because the traditional media "gatekeepers" would have kept them locked out, despite the fact that they had a lot of valuable expertise and information to share with the public.

So - we felt pretty good about what we had accomplished. We had gotten some real substantial entrepreneurs and industry leaders in entertainment, finance, personal development, health and fitness, real estate and law, among other fields, the kind of credibility usually reserved for the media elite. Their professional profiles and revenues had both risen as a result. We had also created and now had at our disposal numerous offline and online media channels to ensure our deserving clients would be able to reach their desired target audiences.

Still…something was missing from the equation. And, as time went by, we began to realize we had done things slightly backwards. We were using a "reverse-dessert" recipe. By that, we mean that we had completely bypassed the cake and, instead, first made the *icing*. Now, don't get us wrong, people loved that icing – it was definitely sweet – but it needed something stronger underneath to hold onto. We discovered what should go into that "cake" almost by accident.

Here's how: When we were first starting out, it was important when we did a "live" talk in front of a crowd, that we introduce ourselves. Of the two of us, Nick was the one who did the most traveling and did the most talks. He made sure to always begin his presentation by sharing his own personal story – about how he started in the music business, producing albums and working with top recording artists. His exposure to that level of creativity and media exposure made him want to apply those concepts to the business world as well (something we obviously followed through on by creating our "Celebrity Branding" methodology).

Well, after a while, Nick didn't think he needed to tell that story over and over again; he thought it didn't add anything and he dropped it. However, he began to notice that people were not as *responsive* to his overall talks. He wasn't getting as many audience members coming up to talk to him afterwards as he had before – and, ultimately, not getting as much business. He finally put his finger on what might have caused the drop-off in interest - and decided to put his personal "mini-bio" back in his talks. The reaction immediately improved.

It was our first inkling that, when it came to branding, a client's *story* was as important as a client's expertise. The more we tried it out, the more we saw that this was indeed the case; when we told the right story, audiences (and customers) were much more receptive and much more eager to "buy" us. Demonstrating knowledge and capability were great, but not enough to really "seal the deal"; an effective story, however, caused a deeper and more meaningful bond to occur. As we began to look at it even closer, we realized that at the end of the day, **your story is your brand**. Or to put it another way, branding is simply storytelling, and any form of media is just a medium to tell that story. Simple, but as we soon found out, very profound.

We saw that we needed to get our recipe in the right order: Create our "cake" (the story) first and then add the "icing" (the rest of our systems to establish credibility and visibility). The impact would be twice as powerful - which was more than a little exciting, considering how well we were already doing with our current methods.

We came to call this new concept, "StorySelling™" – and it's now the cornerstone of our approach, simply because it *is* so effective. And once we looked into *why* stories were so effective, we were *completely* blown away. So blown away that we decided this book needed to be written.

Inside these pages, we're going to reveal the secrets behind Story-Selling, the scientific and sociological reasons stories work, and some detailed case studies of how we've used the concept to great success at our agency. We're also going to explain why StorySelling™ is critical to any branding effort – and why your business efforts *must* include telling the right tantalizing tale in order to attract a devoted following.

Bottom line: We're about to tell you a story about stories – and we guarantee you'll be sitting on the edge of your seat throughout it.

ACT I

THE POWER OF STORYSELLING™
How It Works

"Stories are how we think. They are how we make meaning of life...Stories are how we explain how things work, how we make decisions, how we justify our decisions, how we persuade others, how we understand our place in the world, create our identities, and define and teach social values."

~ Dr. Pamela Rutledge,
*Director, Media Psychology
Research Center*

CHAPTER 1

STORYSELLING™
In The Beginning

So, one day, Gronk was headed back home after a particularly good hunt. As he dragged a dead bison behind him, he whistled a happy tune, not realizing it was a few notes away from being the future theme of "Wheel of Fortune." The family would be happy with the dinner he was bringing back. Yep, 15,324 B.C. was shaping up to be a great year.

As he entered his cave, he left the bison out front for the women to clean and cook. He took off his hunting fur and put on his evening fur, then laid down on the dirt for a little relaxation; he needed to unwind with some entertainment. Then he remembered TV hadn't been invented yet, there wasn't even radio, nor would there be a *New York Times* crossword puzzle to solve for about 16,000 years or so. The Nintendo system he built out of rocks also wasn't a whole gang of fun either.

So…Gronk stared at the drab, dark cave wall by his head and sighed. A bunch of kids ran up to him and grunted at him inquisitively, pointing at the dead bison, whose festive aroma was attracting attention. Gronk knew they wanted to know how he had managed to kill the creature, but he was beat and way too tired to try to invent a language to tell them how. Still…they kept right on grunting at him.

Gronk rolled his eyes and got to his feet. He tried to act out the hunt. But he wasn't a gifted physical performer. And the kids were now grunting more and more impatiently. He finally spotted a familiar stone on the ground by his foot. He was screwing around the other night and had scraped it across the wall – and it left a mark behind it.

Huh. Gronk wondered if he could make a whole bunch of marks on the wall. Maybe he could even make the marks look like the bison…? He picked up the stone and started scraping it on the wall. The kids' grunts were now very confused. They watched spellbound as Gronk found his inner artist and sketched out a crude bison – well, if you squinted the right way, it looked like a bison anyway. Then Gronk sketched out himself spearing the bison from behind.

The kids grunted excitedly. This was a show they would never forget.

In the coming days, everyone from caves all around town began to stop by Gronk's pad to see his growing gallery of bison kills. In the meantime, Gronk had discovered other colored stones that he added to his "palette." His drawings became more sophisticated. His last bison kill picture had gotten "Four Bones" from the local critic.

Then finally, he made the big breakthrough. He wanted to show the steps to a bison kill, but he couldn't do it in just one picture. So he drew *a series* of pictures depicting the beginning, the middle and the end of the hunting strategy. Gronk had just made his historical mark as *the inventor of the story*.

Too bad a rhino ran him off a cliff the next day.

Okay, so we can't be sure that's the way the first story came out – or that a caveman named Gronk was the brains behind it –

but, historically, the first physical evidence of storytelling comes from drawings like the ones just described that were found in caves in southwestern France; the carbon dating does indeed age them at roughly 17,000 years old.

But, just because we had a little fun with our cave drawing narrative, the basic concept is pretty hard to argue with; the first stories were simply a matter of necessity. They were the easiest way to *explain* events that had happened. Man is a time-based creature; we understand things as they happen in a sequence because that's how we experience life.

A story simply replicates that life experience. To boil a story down to the essentials: This happened, then *that* happened, and then, because of those things…a *final* thing happened. If that sounds simple, it's because it is – and that simplicity is what has given stories their power right from the opening chapter of human history.

FROM THE CAVE TO THE COMPUTER

As we noted, cave drawings were the first way we came up with to tell a story. Those later evolved in hieroglyphics in ancient Egypt. Of course, you can only tell so much with pictures – and it can be a real drag having to sketch everything out. That's why, around 3000 B.C., the Sumerian tribes in southern Mesopotamia developed the first primitive *writing,* which they called "cuneiform." Suddenly, stories could be written in more detail – and that eliminated the guesswork involved in trying to figure out what those scrawls on those walls were trying to say.

The next big evolution in storytelling was in 700 B.C., when the first *printed* story that we're aware of shows up: It was called "The Epic of Gilgamesh" – and no, Gilgamesh wasn't one of those Japanese movie monsters like Godzilla and Gamera. As a matter of fact, he was one of the first rulers of what we now know as Iraq, and, while he didn't have weapons of mass destruction, he *was* regarded as two-thirds of a god (which is better than nothing). Copies of this story managed to spread all across Europe and Asia.

Of course, most people back then couldn't read or write, which is why most stories were spread by simple word-of-mouth. This created a "survival of the fittest" process where the best stories ended up having an abnormally long shelf life, even though they only existed in oral form.

For example, around 500 B.C., a fellow named Aesop was walking around delivering a great many memorable "fables" – stories that always had a moral lesson (or, as we call it today, a "takeaway"). Aesop's storytelling prowess was so awesome that his tales were repeated over and over, from generation to generation – and it wasn't until *three hundred years later,* after its author was long dead and buried, that *Aesop's Fables* were actually written down and distributed. Homer, the guy who brought us *The Iliad* and *The Odyssey,* was dead for *five* hundred years before anyone bothered to write his stuff down.

However, the fact remained that these and other powerful stories *refused to die.* There was something meaningful about them that motivated people to not only spread these stories far and wide, but also to hand them down to their children, and their children's children.

That's how The Bible came to be, of course – hundreds of years of oral storytelling, finally resulted in holy men putting these tales together in the Old and New Testaments. The Bible also became the centerpiece of the next phase of storytelling, when Johannes Gutenberg created what we know as the modern printing press. Of course, it's not so modern anymore due to computers.

Which brings us to the 20th Century, where we saw the most rapid and transformational change in storytelling. What we now know as "Old Media" was brand new then – movies, radio and television were suddenly able to tell us stories in new and exciting ways. And, of course, the 21st Century has brought even more incredibly storytelling tools, through the explosion of "New Media" – online video, social media, blogs, websites and more.

Stories are more important to us than ever – and more volatile than ever. An effective narrative, even if it's found in a simple YouTube video, can quickly go viral throughout the world – indicating the public is feverishly searching for great stories more than at any other time in history. Aesop, if he were around today, would no doubt have his own Tumblr blogsite that would attract millions (especially if his fables featured the Kardashian family instead of turtles and birds).

Maybe we seek out more stories than ever before simply because we have instant access to more of them than ever before. The shrinking sizes of digital files, combined with the increased storage power of our mobile devices, means we can literally carry around a library with us in the palm of our hands. And that trend will only accelerate:

For example, George Church, the genetics professor at Harvard Medical School, appeared on "The Colbert Report" in October of 2012, and handed the host a tiny vial with a small piece of paper inside – which had a dot circled in red on it. Church, who was promoting a book, explained that he had used a code to create a DNA version of the three hundred page manuscript, and then made 20 million DNA copies of it.

All 20 million copies of that book were contained inside the red dot on the piece of paper - which was about the size of the point of a Sharpie marker.

THE DYNAMIC DUO OF STORYTELLING AND STORYSELLING™

This book is about StorySelling™, however – not storytelling. The difference? With StorySelling™, you're not just trying to relate a series of events: You're using storytelling to advocate a point of view; it's more selective and more designed to elicit a specific response.

For example, StorySelling™ has been central to the development of the world's greatest religions and philosophies; whether it's Buddha sitting under the Bodhi tree for 49 days or L. Ron Hubbard claiming aliens once walked the earth. Mystical, fanciful legends are created and retold to inspire followers to subscribe to certain belief systems. Countries also spawn their own narrow historical narratives to promote patriotism. Let's return to Iraq – remember, how in Baghdad, there were giant paintings of Saddam Hussein everywhere in the city, some several stories tall? Not to mention the giant statue of him that we ended up pulling down after we invaded? Saddam was doing his own StorySelling™ – to convince his people that he was a great ruler who deserved to be worshipped.

The same thing happens here in America, to a limited extent. For example, the heroic tales of such towering figures as George Washington, Abraham Lincoln and Martin Luther King Jr. don't dwell on such unpleasant facts like Washington had slaves, Lincoln had a crazy wife and MLK was rumored to stray outside his marriage; that stuff is for students of history. The rest of us like to focus on legends that make us feel good about our country.

Yes, it's the harsh truth: *we all like to be on the receiving end of StorySelling™.*

We humans have a tribal mentality – and we like to feel part of a narrative that's bigger than us. We look for stories to define who we are, what we're all about and where we belong. That's why the most notable leaders throughout history have utilized powerful stories to both attract and maintain followers. Storytelling and StorySelling™ have been partners from the very get-go.

Let's go back to Gronk and his cave drawings. Undoubtedly, his other cave buds had their hunting strategy. Gronk, however, would have thought *his* way was the best - and so he would have chosen that method to immortalize on the cave wall. Making that choice meant Gronk was StorySelling™ his "Foolproof Method of Bagging a Bison."

Of course, StorySelling™ could get pretty crazy in the early days. Before there was science, it was difficult for people to explain what made lightning happen. Or thunder. Or where the sun came from in the morning and where it went at night. Nobody knew why it got cold in the winter and hot in the summer – and no one could explain why there was a lot of food available sometimes and so little other times that some would actually die of starvation.

Enter the storyteller – or, to take it a step further, the Story*Seller.* A gifted storyteller would have enough imagination to invent a story involving mythical "gods" to explain the unexplainable. This immediately gave this person a great deal of power – if he could explain the forces that ruled everyone's daily lives, he held the keys to life and death (even though he himself knew he just made the whole thing up).

So the StorySeller would use this fact to his advantage – and create superstitions, rituals, morals, traditions, rules, codes, and laws that others would immediately adhere to, because they were frightened of what happened if they "displeased the gods." The better and more enthralling his stories were, the more the StorySeller could control everyone else's behavior. He could make himself a High Priest – and everyone in the community would not only treat him in the highest regard, but also make sure his standard of living was above theirs.

Like any dominant methodology, this type of StorySelling™ could obviously be employed towards a higher purpose – or an evil one. It could be used to create a happy and harmonious living environment, where everyone abides by moral laws that protect the common good - or it could be used simply to grab power and keep the population captive to that power.

The 20th Century was filled with these kinds of "StorySellers." Think of Karl Marx, creating "The Communist Manifesto" – and all of Russia falling to his subsequent revolution. Think of Adolf Hitler writing his book "Mein Kampf," quickly ascending to leadership and almost conquering all of Europe.

More benignly, Senator John F. Kennedy "wrote" (with the help of a ghostwriter) "Profiles in Courage," a best seller which won the Pulitzer Prize and boosted his profile in time for his Presidential run in 1960. Similarly, Barack Obama prepared for political life by writing his own best-seller, "Dreams from My Father," which reflected on his life and philosophy up until that point and introduced himself to the public at large, who might not have been all that crazy about electing a guy with the middle name of "Hussein."

Today, political StorySelling™ is still at a fever pitch; in America, several networks have their own strong narratives in place, which serves their respective audience by consistently validating their particular beliefs, often at the expense of what some would consider a more fact-based "truthful" and traditional journalistic approach. They are true "StorySellers" rather than storytellers.

STORYSELLING™ YOUR LIFE

StorySelling™ isn't just employed for such lofty grandiose goals as creating gods and toppling countries, however. Most of us use StorySelling™ in one form or another every day of our lives in every kind of trivial situation. See if these lines sound familiar…

"I meant to call you, but the boss gave me all this work at the last-minute…"

"Officer, I swear, the light had just turned yellow…"

"The dog ate my homework."

Yes, technically, we call them "excuses," but they are also "stories" – stories designed to help us avoid an unpleasant consequence of something we did (or didn't do). But our personal StorySelling™ skills can also be employed to higher and more important life goals:

"Remember the first time we met?"

"I knew the minute I saw you, I wanted to marry you."

"Whenever I heard your name, I got a special tingling feeling…"

We *also* "create" narratives for our relationships – especially the romantic ones. We reinforce them with each other – and also relate them to friends and family, so they feel good about the person we've decided to be with. That means we embroider our relationship stories with as much loving detail as possible – and leave out the parts like that time we screamed at each other in that mall parking lot...

There are many, many other occasions in our lives where we want to put forth the most positive narrative as possible, such as:

- *Interviewing for a job*
- *Trying to get a new client*
- *Christmas dinner with relatives*
- *Applying for a loan or trying to borrow money*
- *Meeting someone new and important*

And those are only the tip of the iceberg. Socially, professionally and romantically, we almost always want to "StorySell" the most positive version of ourselves. Our StorySelling™, in these instances, may not actually involve deception, but it will probably be, at the least, guilty of "the sin of omission" – by avoiding anything that might be perceived as a negative by the other party.

But the question remains...why is StorySelling™ so effective? Why does a good story sometimes cause people to change their beliefs, their behavior and even their entire life perspective? And why do we trust the StorySeller to the point where we allow that to happen?

As we noted earlier in this chapter, there are very good scientific reasons for this – and we'll be sharing those reasons in the next chapter.

CHAPTER 2

THE SCIENCE OF STORYSELLING™
Hitting the "Love Hormone"

So the marketing director of one of the biggest fast food chains in the world had a problem on his hands. His biggest competitive advantage was probably that his food was a whole lot healthier than his rivals' – but his research was pretty clear that promoting that advantage wasn't going to do a whole lot for the chain's sales.

He knew he could go out there with all sorts of statistics and health information and make the case – but, frankly, all those numbers would just bore consumers, who only considered stopping in at one of his eateries for a quick meal when they were short on either money or time, or possibly both.

That meant the marketing director wasn't particularly excited when a Chicago franchisee found out about some guy who dropped a lot of pounds by only eating their food and took the story to the chain's ad agency. Again, they weren't promoting themselves as the fast food equivalent of Jenny Craig or anything like that, so what good would that do? Not only that, but this kind of campaign could get the company in legal hot water.

Their lawyers were warning that they could be in for a ton of liability lawsuits should they make any kind of informal health claims or promises.

The ad agency was insistent that this was a great idea, however. They put together a legal disclaimer that the lawyers could live with. So the marketing director finally sighed and agreed to try a regional test campaign.

Jared Fogle, a guy who lost 245 pounds eating the exact same Subway sandwich every day for months, appeared in his first commercial on January 1st, 2000 – and the next thing he knew Oprah was booking him on her show. The marketing director was astounded by the instant success of the campaign and it was soon rolled out nationally.

During the next ten years, Subway's sales doubled, the chain moved up from being the number four fast food franchise (After McDonalds, Burger King and Wendy's) to become number three (displacing Wendy's) and Jared became a minor celebrity.

Not only that, but every time Subway tried to dump Jared from their advertising, their sales suffered. The first time, in 2005, sales immediately fell by 10%. Jared's story was now Subway's – and it made them billions of dollars in the process.

The success of the Jared campaign is surely based on the premise of our first book, *Celebrity Branding You*: "People buy people." When you effectively promote a real, living, breathing human being that people can connect with, as opposed to dry facts, the audience is going to be a lot more responsive just because of that "human touch." And when you combine that personality with a compelling story, you've hit a marketing home run.

That's just what Subway did with Jared, who's a perfect example of the potential StorySelling™ holds for a business. He crystal-lized for consumers what ordinary nutritional information could never have accomplished; he provided an authentic story that visually demonstrated the benefit of eating at Subway (as long as, of course, you took it easy on the mayo, bacon and cheese!).

But why was Jared necessary to make that kind of impact? Why couldn't simple and verifiable health facts deliver the same message – and, in turn, motivate the same rise of sales? For that answer, we have to examine the science of StorySelling™. Don't worry, you won't have to memorize any formulas and there won't be a test – but you will learn some very surprising secrets about the power of stories.

YOUR BRAIN AND STORIES
A LOVE AFFAIR

We talked in the last chapter about just how dominant stories are throughout all of human history. People have always utilized whatever medium they had at their disposal – everything from cave drawings to drums to books to YouTube videos – to _tell_ _stories_. As we've seen, some stories were considered so vital that they were passed down solely through the spoken word for hundreds and hundreds of years, before someone finally had the ability to write them down.

The question remains – _why_ do we like stories so much? Actually, change that – because we don't just _like_ stories – we _love_ them.

Literally.

Researchers at the Center for Neuroeconomics Studies at Claremont Graduate University, in Claremont, California,[1] discovered that stories activate the oxytocin hormone in our brains – this is actually _called_ "the love hormone" by the scientific community. That's because it's associated with romantic attachment, human bonding...and yes, sex. In other words, stories are way sexy. Even when they themselves are very far from it.

---

1 Jorge A. Barraza and Paul J. Zak, "Empathy toward Strangers Triggers Oxytocin Release and Subsequent Generosity," June 2009, Annals of the New York Academy of Sciences

Dr. Paul Zak, one of the Claremont researchers, showed volunteers a video that told a story about a four-year-old boy with terminal brain cancer – and also showed the same group a video of the same length about a four-year-old boy going to the zoo without any real narrative to it. Those that watched the first video had a 47% higher level of the love hormone. "Of all the stimuli we've developed that release oxytocin, this one was the best," said Zak of the story experiment.

Why do stories trigger that kind of reaction? Other research suggests that it happens because we identify with whoever the story is about – and put ourselves in their shoes. After all, we're all people – and we all experience the same fears, desires, joys and ambitions.

More fun with brain scanning confirms that this is true. Jeffrey Zacks of Washington University in St Louis, Missouri ran functional magnetic resonance imaging (fMRI) scans on people reading a story or watching a movie[2] – and discovered that, when the main character encountered a situation, it activated the same parts of the brain in the subjects that would have responded if *they themselves* had been in the same predicament in real life. And it didn't matter if the story was read or experienced through a movie or a video – it was the content of the story itself that provoked the reaction.

We are addicted to stories in a very real sense - and here's more research that proves it. Read Montague of Virginia Tech University in Blacksburg and William Casebeer of the US Defense Advanced Research Projects Agency (DARPA) in Arlington, Virginia,[3] analyzed how listening to a story affects the brain's reward centers – the parts that respond to such wonderful things as sex, good food and drugs. Casebeer's conclusion? "If I were a betting man or woman, I would say that certain types of stories might be addictive and, neurobiologically speaking, not that dif-

2 Gerry Everding, "Readers Build Vivid Mental Simulations of Narrative Situations, Brain Scans Suggest," January 26th, 2009, phys.org
3 Jessica Marshall, "Gripping Yarns," *New Scientist*, February 12, 2011

ferent from taking a tiny hit of cocaine," says Casebeer.

Simply put, strong stories key into our emotions in a deep and profound way; we identify with them in a way we don't identify with raw data. That's why Jared's miracle sandwich diet was so effective for Subway - and also why raw black and white information wouldn't have been. Consumers could *see* that eating at Subway actually caused a person like them to lose weight – and, most importantly, could see it working for *them*. They identified with Jared – and it made for a very rewarding experience for their reward centers.

SPLITTING THE DIFFERENCE

Beyond the emotional component, however, stories actually accomplish a critical *function* for our brains. Believe it or not, *we need them to figure out our lives.*

Let's switch up researchers to find out just why this is - and examine the work of neuroscientist Michael Gazzaniga from the University of California, Santa Barbara. Gazzaniga has done incredible research in the whole right brain – left brain arena. He's the person who discovered that the mind's right side was more artistic, creative and visual, while the left side was more verbal and intellectual (and he did this at the ripe old age of 25).[4]

Now, given that the right side of the brain was the artistic and creative half, that half would be the one that would naturally respond best to stories in whatever form they take, right?

Wrong – and this is where it gets interesting.

You see, Gazzaniga also discovered that you could actually *separate* the left side of the brain from the right, and the left side wouldn't suffer any loss in I.Q. points. Don't ask us how he found that out, we're afraid it will sound like a horror movie we definitely do *not* want to watch. Ever.

---

4 Benedict Carey, "Decoding the Brain's Cacophony," *The New York Times*, October 31st, 2011

But something about the brain's ability to seemingly function the same, even when split in half, confused the good doctor. It didn't add up – if the different sides of our brains acted that independently, what accounted for our unity of thought, action and purpose?

To find out, Gazzaniga used his access to people who had had surgery to disconnect communication between the two halves of their brains (this is done sometimes for severe epileptics, for example). What he discovered was equally revolutionary.

Whatever information he gave to the right side of the brain, the *left* side of the brain would then work overtime to explain. The left side, through storytelling, concocted narratives to make sense of random information. More research confirmed his initial results: Gazzinga began to call the left side of our brains, "The Interpreter" – because a big part of its job is to put together individual facts to make a complete mental "picture." In other words, the artistic half of our brains doesn't come up with the stories – the intellectual half does. And not as a creative pursuit – *but just as a way to make sense of what was happening all around it.*

Think about your own daily life. Think about how many times you try to explain to yourself (or to someone who's with you) something random that happens. For example…you hear a random piece of gossip about someone acting strangely. You immediately try to connect the dots to solve the riddle of why that person acted out of character, and come up with excuses like, …"They're getting a divorce," …"They're on drugs," or maybe, …"They lost their job."

Or…your car makes a funny noise on the way home from the store. You immediately try to formulate an explanation in your head for why it's making that sound. Needs an oil change. Maybe the muffler's loose. Or…you watch TV shows like "CSI," "NCIS" or "Bones" — hour-long shows that have a central mystery at their core in each episode. These shows are so popular (just as murder mysteries and detective novels have traditionally been), because the audience is constantly trying to figure out the solution to whatever bizarre crime is being dramatized.

This tendency gets even more intense with a show like "Mad Men" or "Homeland," shows that have an ongoing storyline. Something shocking happens at the end of the episode – and you spend the week trying to concoct the storyline that led up to the cliffhanger (and not just you – there are fifty million people on the internet also blogging and commenting, *also* trying to explain what happened).

Now, the above examples have something very much in common. In all instances, you pretty much *have no idea what the real story is.* But, the sad truth is...*you can't stop your brain from trying to figure it out anyway.*

That's your left side talking. It wants to know. It NEEDS to know.

Remember how, in the last chapter, we talked about how man, pre-science, would make up various "gods" to explain away all kinds of natural happenings? That's because, at that time, humans weren't capable of discovering that the earth was round and it rotated – and *that's* why the sun came up in the morning and sank down in the evening. But they *still had to know why.*

So they made up stuff. They filled in the blanks, just like we do every day.

It may be hard for you to think of Subway's Jared as an ancient god, but, in a sense, he was. He personified Subway's healthy eating possibilities and provided a living explanation of how they might work through his very dramatic weight loss story. He filled in the blanks in a way that had impact. So people bought his StorySelling™ – and, more importantly to the company, they subsequently bought a lot of Subway sandwiches.

OTHER STORY BENEFITS

Stories make us feel good – and they help us explain things (even if we have to make up stuff to do it). But it doesn't stop there - scientists have discovered other valuable advantages that stories deliver to our brains, such as:

- **Survival Benefits**

  Stories are also a way to transmit information that helps us in tricky situations. They can tell you how to react in a dangerous situation, how you should react to people displaying less-than-honorable intentions and inform you about things you don't know a great deal about. Stories also allow us to try out different ideas and scenarios and imagine what happens if we make different choices. Even Jared's story tells us how we can lose weight (if we're willing to eat the "same damn sandwich" every day for a year).

- **Social Glue**

  Stories bring people together and allow them to share the same emotions; they help us socialize and bond as communities. For example, when a popular TV show or movie is around, we all feel we should see it so we can talk about it with friends and relatives who have also seen it; same thing with a big sporting event like the Super Bowl or the World Series, which always has its own narrative (if it doesn't, the sportscasters will give it one anyway!).

Uri Hasson of Princeton University showed different people the same movie and monitored their mental responses[5] – and found the same patterns of neural activity occurred. Other research shows that the brain activity of a person *listening* to a story mirrors that of the person *telling* the story.

By the way, Jared is proof of this social glue aspect as well – he became such a cultural phenomenon that he was parodied on "South Park," which even had a song written about him!

---

5 Ushma Patel, "Hasson Brings Real Life into the Lab to Examine Cognitive Processing," News at Princeton, December 5th, 2011

• A Mental "Time Out"

Stories are also awesome for just good old escapism. Rafi Malach of the Weizmann Institute of Science in Rehovot, Israel, did research[6] that shows that movies can actually suppress activity in the parts of the brain where we try to deal with our ongoing day-to-day problems. With that part "shut down" by an engrossing movie, we're relieved of any anxieties or fear – and are instead focused on a good story that makes us forget about ourselves.

• Fights Terrorism

Well, okay, this claim is only a "maybe."

Remember that guy we mentioned a couple of pages back - William Casebeer of the US Defense Advanced Research Projects Agency (DARPA)? Maybe a question passed through your mind (we're currently *not* monitoring your brain activity, so we can't tell): "Why is a US Defense guy studying stories?"

Remember how we talked about how strong stories are the backbone of a religion? Well, Casebeer thinks the same thing – for example, he believes that belief in a powerful story is what really causes someone to become a suicide bomber. What's more, he believes we can attack that suicide bomber in advance – with a MORE powerful story (and you thought the arms race was dead…), using what Casebeer calls, "counter-narrative strategies."

In his words, "It might be that understanding the neurobiology of a story can give us new insights into how we prevent radicalization, and how we prevent people from becoming entrenched in the grip of a narrative that makes it more likely that they would want to intentionally cause harm to others."

---

6 Kalanit Grill-Spector and Rafael Malach, "The Human Visual Cortex," Department of Psychology and Neuroscience, Stanford University, 2004

(By the way, if you want to see more of your tax dollars at work, you can check out his full report at: http://www.dtic.mil/cgi-bin/ GetTRDoc?AD=ADA521449 .)

As we've hopefully demonstrated in this chapter, a myriad of scientists and researchers have all come up with the same conclusion about stories – that certain ones really *do* answer primal needs that we all need to have met.

That's what makes StorySelling™ so powerful. When done correctly, it hits the human brain with an incredible impact, most of which is felt on a subconscious level. It also activates the pleasure centers of the brain – which makes you want to hear more.

Jared's diet breakthrough saga accomplished all that and more. It made a treat into a health food ("You mean you can lose weight by eating 6-inch subs?") and it created the perception that Subway's food wasn't just good to eat, it was also good *for* you. The campaign was as effective as it could have possibly been, simply because Jared's story was *true* – and yet unbelievable at the same time.

But, wait - did Jared's story actually *need* to be true?

We're about to let you in on another big story secret: The answer is *no* – and in the next chapter, we'll tell you why.

CHAPTER 3

STORYSELLING™ IS BELIEVING
The Truth About Fact and Fiction

So, in January of 1967, Paul McCartney, then-member of the Beatles (we assume you've heard of them), was in a car accident in London. A brief rumor gripped England that Sir Paul was actually killed in the crash. The next month, the official Beatles "fanzine" verified that McCartney was, in fact, alive and well, and life went on as normal - for a while, anyway.

A little over two years later, however, in the autumn of 1969, the stress of superstardom had pulled apart the world's most popular rock group. The Beatles were splitting up, and Paul was spending more and more time in Scotland with his new wife Linda, out of the public eye.

And that's when the weirdness really kicked in. With Paul in hiding for the first time since he and his mates became superstars, the student newspaper at Drake University in Iowa printed a story that seriously asked the question, "Is Beatle Paul McCartney Dead?" The rumor had grown in strength on the campus – and suddenly the students were hunting down clues that had supposedly been placed on the group's most recent albums. For instance, when part of the "Revolution #9" track on *The White Album* was played backwards, a voice said, "Turn me on, dead man." Others swore that, as the end of "Strawberry Fields Forever" faded away, another voice clearly said, "I buried Paul."[1]

Suddenly, Derek Taylor, the Beatles' press rep back in London, was inundated by calls – was Paul in fact deceased? He denied that he was. Because…well, he wasn't.

But then, the rumor made its way to Detroit – where another college newspaper made fun of the gossip by writing a satirical article detailing the "clues" that proved that McCartney was no longer living. Unfortunately, the story was picked up as *fact* by newspapers across the U.S. – and soon the subject was burning up the radio airwaves in New York City, among other major cities.

The "real story" was revealed as this: McCartney had died in that London car crash a few years ago. The Beatles, desperate to continue their success, had replaced him with a guy named William Campbell, the winner of a Paul McCartney look-alike contest, who coincidentally enough, evidently *sounded just like him and had the same incredible musical talent.* Huh?

Three songs were written and released by other rockers about the "death" of Paul. A television special was produced and syndicated nationally, in which a courtroom "trial" was held to decide if Paul was, in fact, dead; F. Lee Bailey, a leading celebrity lawyer at the time, cross-examined "witnesses." The verdict? Well, that was left in the hands of the viewers. And finally, Paul McCartney decided to rise from the dead - and give an interview to *Life* magazine declaring he was alive and well – and just enjoying being "not famous" for the first time in many years.

The rumor finally began to subside, but only after it had been debated all over the world, and recent Beatles songs, and even album photographs and artwork, were rigorously examined to

---

1 John Lennon later revealed, the voice was saying "Cranberry sauce."

uncover "hidden" clues. Even as late as 2010, a mockumentary entitled *Paul McCartney Really Is Dead: The Last Testament of George Harrison?* contained someone claiming to be the late George Harrison on audio tape explaining that the rumor was true. But the person on the tape wasn't George, and Paul, as we write this, is still nowhere near his expiration date.

Now, we will grant you, there have been plenty of movies about look-alikes taking over for famous people. But, as far as we know, there's never been an example of this actually happening in real life – let alone it happening with a worldwide superstar subject to intense media scrutiny who continued to publicly perform and create new music.

So...*how could anyone swallow this story???*

How could anyone believe that someone could quickly and easily take the place of someone as talented and singular as Paul McCartney was at the time? Even while new records featuring his instantly recognizable voice were still being made and released? How could anyone for a minute not only buy this whopper – but continue to spread it all across the globe?

Well, there is a very good reason many people actually believed it (or, at the very least, took it seriously) – and that's because it was *a great story.* And, as we'll see in this chapter, a great story causes people to believe fiction over fact – *because the human brain can't tell the difference.*

Scary? A little bit.

For now, let's find out why this happens – and what it means in terms of StorySelling™.

FACT VERSUS FICTION
WHEN THE TRUTH DOESN'T MATTER

First, though, we want to remind you of a couple of points we made in the last chapter. Point one: Stories aren't necessarily a *creative* process – your brain generates and uses them as a *tool* to explain your life and what's happening around you.

Point two: Good stories hit your brain in its "reward centers" – they activate that "love hormone" we talked about and cause chemical reactions that make you feel good in fundamental ways.

Now, let's apply those two points to the "Paul-is-dead" story and why it developed such a massive following, even though it was patently absurd:

To the first point, the "Paul-is-dead" story *explained* why Beatles fans were suddenly not seeing one of their idols anymore, after nonstop public exposure since the group became famous. After all, everyone knew where his creative partner John Lennon was (this was the period when John was running around with new wife Yoko making headlines with outrageous stunts) and Paul's absence from the spotlight stood out in comparison.

To the second point, the "Paul-is-dead" rumor made those believing the story feel good in the way that "Truthers" (people who believed 9/11 was an "inside government job") and "Birthers" (people who believed that Barack Obama wasn't born in the U.S.) felt good about their conspiracies – even though both those ideas are very distasteful concepts to many people. A fantastic story that seems to have a basis in actual ascertainable "facts" (shaky as those facts might be in reality) gets the listener excited; not only does it make sense of something strange, it also makes believers feel that *they're* in on a secret that has everyone else fooled, and, thus, they feel *smarter* than everyone else. They also feel part of an "inside group" - and that sense of belonging to an exclusive community makes them feel more important.

Primarily for those two reasons, a great story has the ability to "carry your brain away" – literally – through a concept that researchers call *"transportation."* Now, this isn't the kind of transportation that gets you to work or to the supermarket; *this* mode of transportation was discovered by researchers Melanie C. Green and Timothy C. Brock of Ohio State University[2] and it involves just how stories can impact your belief systems – even if those stories aren't necessarily factually accurate.

To quote the researchers, "...the reader loses access to some real-world facts in favor of accepting the narrative world that the author has created. This loss of access may occur on a physical level - a transported reader may not notice others entering the room, for example - or, more importantly, on a psychological level, a subjective distancing from reality. While the person is immersed in the story, he or she *may be less aware of real-world facts that contradict assertions made in the narrative.*"

To put that in plain English, a *compelling story can be more important to someone than the facts.*

Want proof? Okay, then just consider the iconic album cover from the last record the Beatles made together, *Abbey Road* – featuring a photo of the four band members walking single-file across the street. Paul looks very much alive in the picture – except he happens to be barefoot, while the other three are wearing shoes. Other than that, it's a perfectly normal photo.

But NOT so normal when it came to those who had bought into the "Paul-is-dead" conspiracy - here's what *they* saw: The four Beatles dressed to symbolize nothing less than a funeral procession, with John, dressed in white, as the minister, Ringo, dressed in black, as the undertaker, George, in denim jeans and shirt, as the gravedigger and Paul (or, more accurately, Mr. William Campbell, the guy who *looked* like Paul), barefoot and out of step with the others, as the corpse.

Then there was the Volkswagen parked in the background of the photo, which had "28IF" as part of its license plate number – which, naturally to true "Paul-is-dead" conspiracy buffs, signified that Paul would have been 28 years old at that point - *if*

2 Melanie C. Green and Timothy C. Brock, "The Role of Transportation in the Persuasiveness of Public Narratives," *Journal of Personality and Social Psychology,* Vol. 79, No. 5.

he had lived. In other words, all these obscure hidden meanings were more important to believers than the fact that *Paul was actually shown alive and well on the album cover*. And, since this was in an era that was well before Photoshop, it was pretty obvious that the photo was the real deal.

Again, this is just more evidence that the brain can't really distinguish between fact and fiction when a person has decided to buy into a story. As a matter of fact, it actively fights the impulse – because it's more important that *the brain defends the integrity of the story*. This doesn't just apply to scurrilous dead Beatle stories. We all buy into narratives in our everyday lives – and when those narratives are challenged, we push back against the contradictions. How hard we push back depends on how invested we are in the particular story.

Think of someone who's a rabid Republican or Democrat who's confronted with information that contradicts his or her position. How many times have you said to yourself, when having a discussion with that kind of person, "This person is completely irrational – I have to stop arguing, there's no point!" Odds are you're right. The person *is* being irrational – because the overall story he or she wants to believe in is more important than individual facts that conflict with it.

Getting back to the research of Green and Brock, the doctors discovered that it didn't matter if a story was presented as fact or fiction; if the story was compelling enough, if it had enough ability to "transport" people, it would directly impact their beliefs about the subject matter of the story.

And *that's* how someone could see Paul McCartney walking in a contemporary photograph – and still assume it was a big put-up job to send a hidden message about his death. In the words of Green and Brock, "Individuals may believe realistic fictional programs while discounting news reports that seem implausible." As a matter of fact, that sounds a lot like our world today, doesn't it?

WHY STORIES WIN ARGUMENTS

Transportation is the ultimate goal for any good storyteller. And obviously, it should be the goal of a StorySelling™ effort as well. Just as obviously, however, not just *any* story is going to prompt transportation (in later chapters, we're going to dig deeper into what ingredients are needed to create the kinds of story that enable this transformative process to happen).

What we want you to understand in *this* chapter, however, is that StorySelling™ is the most powerful tool you can use to communicate your personal brand and your company brand. All the research is very consistent on this fact (including the studies we've shared with you in these first three chapters): *stories are the best way to make your "argument."*

Why?

For the simple reason that the people hearing (or watching) the story...*don't perceive it as an argument.* Instead, they identify with the leading character (providing he or she is likeable and interesting enough), put themselves in their shoes, feel what they feel and respond to what the story says about that person and the situation. They shut off the questioning part of their brain, as we've discussed, and give themselves over to the story's events and the consequences of those events.

And remember, since we do use stories to explain things, if we accept the narrative, then we will accept the conclusion. If the story is about how a murderer got away because of a court foul-up, we will feel more inclined to favor tougher laws. If the story is about how an innocent man is put on death row, we will feel more inclined to protect the rights of the accused. The story leads us to those ways of thinking not through direct persuasion, but by dramatic license.

We will only change or modify those beliefs so easily, however, if *we don't know an argument is being made.* To us, it's just a story; it's not supposed to mean anything beyond the beginning, middle and end of a tale. And that's how a story's so-called "moral" can sneak up on us and have an impact.

We use stories to process reality. Think about how powerful a statement that is. Think about how, whatever situation we find ourselves in, we must immediately concoct some kind of story to explain it, even though, ultimately, the story may be false. We still need to have something to hang onto until the "real story" is finally revealed.

StorySelling™ becomes invaluable when you want other people to process *your* reality in a memorable, effective way – the way you want them to see you. Think about a trial lawyer doing his closing argument. How does he persuade the jury? Ninety-nine times out of a hundred, he'll frame what he wants the jury to believe in the form of a story – retelling the events crucial to the case in the way he wants them to be perceived.

In a sense, that's exactly what you do for yourself with StorySelling™. You're telling a story about you and/or your business in the way you want them to perceive you. And because it's not seen as straight sales pitch, your audience's guard is significantly lowered and they're more willing to accept what you have to say.

THE VALUE OF AUTHENTICITY

We feel the need to end this chapter with a word about the truth. This chapter may read as if stories are a license to lie – but there is great peril in that approach. Obviously, the "Paul-Is-dead" conspiracy was pretty much dead and buried itself when Paul came out of hiding and began to give interviews. Whoever William Campbell might have been, he couldn't have been good enough to look exactly like Paul *and* sound exactly like Paul, unless someone was doing *Mission: Impossible* for real.

When a big lie is aggressively sold, it's only a matter of time before it does catch up with you. And with social media ready to blow the whistle at the drop of a hat and virally bust you, your window for successful deception is very short – as short as a few minutes, in some cases.

The fact is, even when your StorySelling™ is effective, your audience won't be as heavily invested in your narrative as they are in, say, their religion, their politics or their relationships. That means that, while you *can* achieve "transportation," it's still a tenuous ride that could be quickly derailed - *if* the story you're telling is ultimately a false one.

We'll discuss the secrets of authenticity later in this book – but for now, understand that StorySelling™ offers you your best chance at reaching people on a deep, meaningful level that can genuinely motivate them to buy from you. Long term, however, you can't misuse that power – or it will come back to haunt you in ways you won't want to happen.

This chapter concludes our examination of why stories themselves have such a profound impact on us all. In the next section of the book, we'll be moving on to discuss how to make *your* story as powerful as possible – because you'll find that when you tell the *right* story in the *right* way, you'll have all the science and history we just talked about on your side.

ACT II

THE BUSINESS OF STORYSELLING™
How It Works

"Why storytelling? Simple: Nothing else works."

~ Steve Denning,
Forbes Magazine

CHAPTER 4

STORYSELLING™
The Secret to CELEBRITY
BRANDING® Success

So, Samuel Joseph Wurzelbacher, recently divorced, found himself at a crossroads. He had decided to leave his telecommunications job to return to his roots as a plumber, a trade he had learned during his years in the Air Force. He thought the career move would help him spend more time with his son.

But there was a bigger potential career move looming down his street that he never saw coming.

He was playing football with his boy in his front yard on October 12, 2008, when he saw then-Senator Barack Obama, three days before the final presidential debate with John McCain, campaigning down the block. So Wurzelbacher, a conservative, decided to confront the candidate and strolled down to where the event was taking place. There, he directed a question at Obama about his tax plan – and commented that he thought it might threaten "the American dream." After a brief discussion, Obama wrapped up his response by saying, "…I think when you spread the wealth around, it's good for everybody."

Suddenly, other prominent conservatives were using Obama's

answer to attack him for advocating wealth distribution and what they considered to be socialism – and they lionized Wurzelbacher for putting Obama on the spot.

Just as suddenly, Wurzelbacher was given a new media-driven name – "Joe the Plumber." Not only that, but three days later, Joe the Plumber became a prime subject of the third presidential debate, with McCain mentioning him repeatedly throughout the night and Obama responding by talking directly at the camera as if he was speaking *directly to Wurzelbacher.*

Yes, within 72 hours, the guy who had been just playing football with his kid was now being addressed by name by the President of the United States. Wurzelbacher couldn't believe his newfound fame. He appeared on *Good Morning, America,* the *CBS Evening News with Katie Couric* and Fox News. Retelling his story became one of John McCain's main campaign strategies in the closing weeks; an ad was created by the Republican Party featuring other different small business people looking into the camera and saying, "I'm Joe the Plumber."

McCain put him onstage with him at several campaign stops in Ohio. As a matter of fact, the candidate got so used to having Joe around that he introduced him at one such event that Joe wasn't scheduled to attend. When Joe didn't show, there was an awkward silence as McCain looked around blankly for a moment. He finally said to the crowd, "You're all Joe the Plumber."

McCain might have lost the election, but Wurzelbacher continued to act like a winner. He wrote a book, he became a motivational speaker, and he was hired to appear in commercials. And, in 2012, he came full circle, as Joe the Plumber went from campaign prop to candidate and won the Republican primary for Ohio's 9th District Congressional seat and went on to challenge the Democratic candidate, Marcy Kaptur.

That October day just down the road from his house, Wurzelbacher literally stumbled into one of the most incredible StorySelling™

situations ever; he instantly became the perfect "working class guy" symbol for the Republican Party and was used to create a new narrative for McCain, much as Jared Fogle was for the Subway chain (as we discussed in Chapter 2).

Wurzelbacher's story captures the pure power of StorySelling™ to create a Celebrity Brand – and because his narrative made such an impact, the McCain campaign quickly tried to leverage it to its advantage and inadvertently made Joe the Plumber a star.

In this chapter, we're going to set the stage for the StorySelling™ that could make *you* a star in your field in equally powerful ways. We're going to talk about the four key factors you need to have in place to StorySell effectively – and also about what you need to consider before you implement your StorySelling™ methods.

In StorySelling™, as in many things in life, the first steps are often the most critical ones – and we want to make sure you get off on the right foot.

THE FOUR KEY FACTORS OF STORYSELLING™

As we just mentioned, there are four key factors that, when combined, create the perfect climate for StorySelling™ success. They are:

1) Simplicity

How many stories do we hear in a day? How much information do we end up taking in? The answer to both of those questions is the same: a scary crazy amount. That means if *your* story isn't simple and easy to grasp, most of us, unless we're already intensely interested in the story, aren't going to hang on to it. Our lives are too busy and our minds too cluttered to take in something that's not directly relevant to what we're dealing with at the moment.

2) Authenticity

We are also bombarded with marketing campaigns night

and day – and most of us can smell a sales pitch a mile off. If your story only seems like an effort to get your audience to buy – or, even worse, if it doesn't have the ring of truth – no one is going to take it seriously. The only exception is if that audience has already heavily bought into your StorySelling™ and feels the need to defend it, even in the face of obvious falsehoods (see previous chapter).

3) Visibility

Obviously, the public, or, at the very least, your target audience, has to have access to the story you want to tell. There are a lot of channels you can utilize to deliver your narrative, which we'll discuss later in the book; the point is, you can't expect your potential leads to come to *you*, you have to find a viable way to bring your story to *them*.

4) Relevancy

It also has to be a story that people *want* to hear. For instance, as we noted with Jared's Subway commercials, viewers loved the idea that you could lose weight at a fast food restaurant. Again, we have so many people out there trying to sell us *their* stories that we block out as many as we can, just to keep our sanity. That means your narrative must be one that your audience is predisposed to hear for one reason or another – and that reason should be a powerful one.

Let's return to the story of Joe the Plumber – and review how these factors came into play for Wurzelbacher.

We'll start with *Simplicity* – because this scenario had it in spades. The situation was easy to grasp and instantly arresting: some guy goes up and directly engages one of the two candidates for President of the United States. Not only that, but he gets that candidate to say something that the opposition can immediately leverage against him. The moment was brief, easily replayable across all media channels, and it captured everyone's attention as a real "David and Goliath" moment, in spite of one's political leanings. The only thing threatening that Simplicity? Well,

"Wurzelbacher" is not the simplest name in the world – but that small problem got solved when he was quickly renamed Joe the Plumber, a very memorable moniker, by everyone in the media. What could be simpler – or easier to remember? What better captured his "Average Joe" status?

Authenticity was also present and accounted for. Wurzelbacher wasn't a political plant – he was a dad playing football with his son who took a minute to confront a candidate. He came across as a "real guy" because he was – and he was obviously saying what he personally believed. There wasn't anything phony about the situation or the participants.

Visibility? A no-brainer. The media already had all their cameras on Obama that afternoon and that's how the entire encounter got captured. After the fact, the video of the confrontation between Joe the Plumber and Barack Obama was endlessly shown on cable and network news channels as well as online; anyone following the presidential race couldn't help but see it.

Finally, there's the matter of Relevancy – or, in other words, exactly *who* wanted to hear the story of Joe the Plumber? If you answered, "The American voting public did," well, that's close, but not quite the right answer – the group that actually wanted a story like this, was even desperate for a story like this, was *the Republican Party*. The McCain campaign's poll numbers were bad, they needed some kind of outside boost, and suddenly, they were given the gift of an everyday American articulating their talking points right to Obama's face. McCain's people made sure Joe the Plumber became a media sensation – and both the Right and the Left seized on his story for their own political reasons.

In short, *Wurzelbacher fulfilled a huge and immediate relevant need* – and, because he was authentic, because his story was so simple, and because his story was so visible, the StorySelling™ of Joe the Plumber took flight.

AVOIDING STORYSELLING™ PITFALLS

Now, the overwhelming majority of StorySelling™ cases do not happen this quickly and this powerfully; with Joe the Plumber, there was a perfect convergence of the four key factors we just discussed. It usually takes some time to StorySell a Celebrity Brand. But the four factors we're discussing here still *must* come into play, no matter who the person in question is or at what speed the StorySelling™ process happens.

But here's an important qualifier – just because those four factors are in place, and just because a StorySelling™ opportunity does present itself, *doesn't mean you should follow through on it.*

Wurzelbacher's story initially made people feel good about supporting John McCain – he was a "real guy" and voters could identify with him. Because Joe the Plumber became famous so quickly, however, nobody really knew that much about him – including the McCain campaign. And, as we've seen over and over, when the media spotlight shines intensely on someone who's not prepared for scrutiny, every possible imperfection gets magnified.

For example, someone examined the records and found out that Joe the Plumber wasn't legally licensed to *be* a plumber in Ohio. They also found out he had a lien placed against his house in 2007 because he owed about $1200 in back state taxes.

More damaging for McCain was the fact that Wurzelbacher was far from a seasoned politician – he was still very rough around the edges. For example, he started weighing in on foreign policy and said that "a vote for Obama is a vote for the death of Israel" in an interview with Shepherd Smith on Fox News. When the interview was done, Smith looked directly at the camera and said "Man, it just gets frightening sometimes."

Suddenly, it was clear that Joe the Plumber wasn't going to help McCain expand his base – not if he was going to alienate anchormen even on Fox. Joe the Plumber, it turned out, was no

Average Joe – instead he was a fervent right-winger with opinions that could possibly alienate more people than they attracted.

Again - *just because you can take advantage of a StorySelling™ opportunity doesn't mean you should.* When you set into motion a StorySelling™ narrative that can't sustain itself, you set yourself up for disaster.

The fact is when you do launch StorySelling™ that the public is ready and willing to buy into, you risk more damage than benefit if that narrative *ultimately will defeat itself.* As we've discussed, stories that connect with people hit them in a very deep subconscious place - and that subconscious place gets *very* angry if the story it bought into isn't for real.

For instance, imagine if Subway had hired Jared for their marketing campaign and he immediately started to gain weight: They would have been a laughing stock, the credibility of the weight loss angle would have been totally shot, and sales probably would have plummeted below where they were before Jared appeared on the scene.

As you can see, StorySelling™ is a two-edged sword. It's truly the most powerful weapon in anyone's personal branding arsenal – but *you must be careful which narratives you choose.* Not only that, but once you've picked one that will work long term, you must be committed to remaining *consistent* with that narrative.

Consider the following infamous incidents:

• Tom Cruise jumping up and down on Oprah's couch like a lunatic and, a few days later, lecturing Matt Lauer about psychiatry.

• Mel Gibson spitting out a drunken anti-Semitic screed at a policeman.

• Peewee Herman getting busted in a porn theatre.

All of those moments substantially damaged these stars' careers, because they publicly and severely contradicted their

StorySelling™ narratives. Suddenly, without much warning, Cruise wasn't the cool in-control guy, Gibson wasn't the happy-go-lucky action star, and Peewee was no longer suitable for children. And since their fans had invested so much into those narratives, they felt doubly betrayed when these unpleasant occurrences were publicized by the media.

WHEN NEGATIVES DON'T MATTER

Of course, StorySelling™ contradictions don't have to be fatal – it really depends on how much credit you have in the StorySelling™ bank, so to speak.

For example, here are three historical figures whose StorySelling™ continues to this day, even though they're no longer with us:

• **Mother Teresa** - the nun who traveled all over the globe to help the neediest people in the most poverty-stricken areas of the world.

• **Abraham Lincoln** – the American President who saved the Union, freed the slaves, and paid the ultimate price.

• **Gandhi** – the Indian leader who led his people to independence through non-violent means.

The above names conjure up strong, straightforward narratives that are simple, authentic, and still relevant, because these three people went beyond the call of duty to deal with issues that still haunt us today. They also remain highly visible through movies, books, television documentaries and school courses. They not only represent the four key factors of StorySelling™ in very powerful ways, they also represent the best of humanity. They make the overwhelming majority of us feel *good* about being human beings; we *want* to believe in their stories.

Of course, if you examined their actual lives a little more closely, you would find the usual human contradictions and complexities that all of us share. For example, did you know…

- Mother Teresa's orphanages were investigated for abuse and neglect?[1]

- Lincoln's attitudes towards race were so confused (as anyone's in the 1800's would be) that one prominent 1960's historian called him a "white supremacist?" [2]

- Gandhi in his later years slept naked with his grandniece to test his willpower (a test we hoped he passed!)?[3]

Now, all of the above facts are true – but these people's legends are so powerful that a few potentially scandalous pieces of trivia can't do them much harm. We want to believe in them too much and they did too much good. But…you don't have to be Abraham Lincoln to keep your image a positive one.

A little while ago, we asked you to imagine what would have happen if Jared had quickly put on some pounds right after Subway had hired him. Well, the fact of the matter is he *did* pork up – ten years into his run as a Subway spokesman. There were even a few ads where Jared's waistline was disguised by big bulky coats.

Subway, showing its skill at StorySelling™, actually turned this into a *positive* – as they had him train for the New York Marathon, which gave them an entirely new narrative to StorySell with their sandwich star and also guaranteed that he would again be svelte and commercial-ready.

Subway could get away with all that just because it *had* been a decade since Jared had signed on – that was more than enough time to prove his weight loss story had been for real. People are willing to deal with a lapse or contradiction in a StorySelling™ narrative as long as it's not too severe and it's addressed in a positive way.

1 "Sins of the Missions," *The Guardian*, October 14th, 1996
2 Bennett Jr., Leronne, *Forced Into Glory: Abraham Lincoln's White Dream*, pp.35 -42, (2000) Johnson Publishing Company
3 Parekh, Bhikhu C., *Colonialism, Tradition and Reform: An Analysis of Gandhi's Political Discourse*, (1999) Sage Publishers

Just like with any other powerful force, StorySelling™ is awesome to use – as long as you can maintain some control over it. John McCain couldn't do that with Joe the Plumber – but, ironically, Joe the Plumber could control it on *his* behalf, as he moved forward with his StorySelling™ narrative to become a media personality in his own right after the election and to this day.

Now – how do you become the "hero" of your own StorySelling™ narrative? How do you capture the imagination of your audience?

Turn the page and find out!

CHAPTER 5

YOUR STORYSELLING™ JOURNEY
Keying into The Ultimate Story

Abandoned by his parents at birth, the young hero was raised by a kindly, humble couple in a small village. The father schooled the boy in the ways of alchemy, showing him how to put to work earthly forces every day in combinations that made astonishing things happen.

The boy was transfixed by his father's talents. And he was further entranced when he met another boy, an aspiring alchemist, whose talents took the art to a whole new level. Together they discussed creating wondrous things. The hero's mind filled with possibilities that the alchemist had never dreamed of – together, they could achieve much.

But the young hero regularly got in trouble. His mind blocked out the conventional teachings of the community and his irreverent attitude towards authority caused him to question the tried and true – the very qualities that fueled his visionary power. Disillusioned, the hero sought to find higher meaning in distant lands, where he experimented with magic potions that changed his consciousness in profound ways. He further sought the advice and mentorship of gifted mystics who would open up new worlds of thought to the young hero. Refreshed and reenergized, he returned to his homeland, determined to discover the destiny that he felt was calling to him – loudly and insistently. He reunited with the alchemist and committed himself to his dreams.

The hero had many early successes – but found it difficult to manage his newfound power. More ominously, the young hero also struggled with the darkness that still lurked in his own consciousness – he found himself at war not only with himself, but with those around him. Still, the hero was besieged with followers who gifted him with riches and accolades. He became the unofficial ruler of the community – and was soon overwhelmed with his new fame and the obligations it entailed.

Desperate for help, the hero took on a clever apprentice, wise to the ways of the world and able to continue to communicate with the hero's followers in his place. The apprentice was untrustworthy, however, and lusted after the hero's power; he turned the hero's followers against him and the hero was exiled from the community he had created. The hero, banished to obscurity, was at his low point. His reputation was destroyed and his magic had been stolen.

And then a strange thing happened. Freed of his responsibilities, the hero's spirit grew lighter. He rekindled his youthful passion – and began to work with other alchemists to take his visions to an entirely new level. Meanwhile, the apprentice who had usurped the hero's mystical throne found whatever magic the hero had left behind was weakening. The people turned against him – and he too was banished.

As the hero's followers began to hear whispered tales of the hero's new achievements, they asked him to return to where he belonged – promising to honor him and allow him to continue to pursue his visions there for the rest of his life. The hero gladly returned and gifted the people with more magic than they had ever imagined possible. The community was prosperous and fruitful.

And we do mean "fruitful." Because that community's name was Apple. And the hero's name?

Steve.

THE SECRET OF THE ULTIMATE STORY

No, the preceding saga was not a lost chapter from the *Lord of the Rings* trilogy – it was actually a short biography of Steve Jobs with a bit of a mystical translation, which we'll explain later in this chapter.

Now, we went to all this trouble for a reason – and that's because, in this chapter, we're going to reveal exactly *why* Steve Jobs' story is so compelling to so many people (probably the most compelling business bio in recent history, to be honest) – and what elements of his story you should be employing in *yours*. In other words, we're going to begin to detail the actual storytelling that goes into effective StorySelling™.

And we're going to start by revealing the major storytelling secrets discovered by a man named Joseph Campbell. If you haven't heard of Campbell, that's okay. But you've probably heard of two of his biggest fans – George Lucas and Steven Spielberg, two of Hollywood's all-time great storytellers who studied Joseph Campbell's works and put his principles into action.

Result? Some of the most successful movies ever made, especially the Lucas *Star Wars* movies, which, more than any other film series, demonstrate the validity of Campbell's findings (and, not-so-coincidentally, are the highest-grossing movies of all time – with the Disney company recently paying *over four billion dollars* to Lucas for the rights to make more of them).

So let's talk about Joseph Campbell – the man who discovered what we call "The Ultimate Story." Campbell, who passed away in 1987, was a mythologist who studied the world's greatest stories – the stories that had been passed down from generation to generation, as discussed in Chapter 1. These are the legends and myths that our ancestors told about heroes, gods and monsters, as well as the stories that informed religions, held together cultures and inspired movements.

And here's the startling fact he discovered about all of them; they all basically *told the same story*. The versions, details and the names, of course, changed – but all the narratives followed a certain pattern that was set in stone…well, back in the Stone Age.

Campbell called this story "The Hero Myth" or "Monomyth"; we like to think of it as "The Ultimate Story," because it's the tale mankind likes to tell more than any other. It generates an incredibly strong psychological pull that's irresistible to an audience – which is why Hollywood's biggest filmmakers like to use The Ultimate Story in their epics. And even though those movies may seem fantastic and completely irrelevant to our lives (as the *Star Wars* movies would seem to be), they still hit our brains in that sweet spot we talked about in Chapter 2.

But *why* do we react to them so strongly? What makes us get so involved with a story set in outer space with spaceship dogfights, princesses and giant furry sidekicks? Simple. The plot of The Ultimate Story actually reflects *universal concerns that all of us face throughout our own lives.* Yes, the conflicts may be taking place in outer space, but they're still similar to challenges we deal with here on Mother Earth. And we want to see the "hero" of The Ultimate Story conquer his problems and succeed – because that gives us hope that we can do the same. His win becomes our win. That's why the Ultimate Story has such a profound effect on all of humanity – and also why it will have a profound effect on *your* audience.

THE NINE STAGES OF THE ULTIMATE STORY
THE HERO'S JOURNEY

It's time to reveal the basic plot of The Ultimate Story. There is *no question* it will seem familiar to you – you've seen countless variations of it, as almost every successful story conforms to its parameters. At the same time, you may think to yourself, "This has *absolutely nothing* to do with me or my business." We just ask that you stick with us, because, later in this chapter, we're going to show you why it absolutely does.

To explain The Ultimate Story, we've created an outline of it, based on Campbell's book, *The Hero with a Thousand Faces*. Although his Ultimate Story has seventeen stages, we've condensed, combined and simplified them down to nine for the StorySelling™ process. They are:

1) **The Ordinary:** We are introduced to our "hero" in his home environment. This is usually a very typical or even impoverished place. At this point, the hero is as much of a "normal" person as possible, so the story listener can identify with him as closely as possible (quick note: for simplicity's sake, we're going to refer to our hero as a guy, but we are definitely aware how heroic women can be!). What begins to make him extraordinary is…

2) **The Calling:** The hero realizes, or is told, what his "destiny" is. It seems intimidating - maybe too much for him to handle or something that simply isn't to his liking, which is why he makes…

3) **The Refusal:** The hero turns away from his calling at first. It seems like there's no way he will accept what it appears he is pre-ordained to do, which is why it's necessary for…

4) **The Intervention:** Something significant steps in to change his mind. It could be a supernatural experience, an older and wiser mentor or some seemingly-random event. Whatever it is, it turns his thinking around so that he embraces…

5) **The Beginning:** The hero answers the calling and begins to gather resources and helpers to fulfill it; he also begins to acquire enemies in the process. He gathers what he

needs to fulfill his "quest," but doesn't quite reach his goal, because he must first face…

6) **The Challenge:** The hero goes as far as he can in this initial phase, until he comes to a standstill. Before he can go further, he must overcome something either significant that's either internal or external, or, more likely, both. But before that can happen, things get even worse, because of…

7) **The Loss**: A horrible event causes a massive setback. It looks like all is lost and that the hero's destiny will never be fulfilled, until…

8) **The Rebirth:** He finds a way to renew his motivation and abilities, perhaps even take them to a whole new level. He is "reborn" and ready to continue his "quest."

9) **The Return:** The hero comes back, better than ever, and fulfills his goals, which helps everyone around him. In other words, a very happy ending.

And that's it. Sounds like a great movie to watch with the kids, right? Well, it's much more than that…

…because, believe it or not, no matter what you do or what product or service you provide, *elements of this Ultimate Story will apply to you and can be utilized to StorySell you.* There's a reason this Ultimate Story has been so popular over the ages – and that's because, as we already noted, it contains elements that are common to every human experience, including yours.

There's a big reason why Steve Jobs became such a revered figure in our time – *his life actually did mirror this Ultimate Story.* He became the stuff of legend to the business world (and even to consumers who love Apple – how many times have you heard them referred to as "fanatics?"). Now, you might say that was only because of his massive success, but there are other individuals who have comparable business achievements whose names you're probably not even familiar with. It's his *story* that really grabs people – his autobiography is still a huge best seller.

The fact is Steve Jobs lived a life that unknowingly fulfilled all the requirements of Campbell's Ultimate Story. And we're about to prove it.

THE NINE STAGES OF STEVE JOBS

Let's go back to the story with which we opened this chapter – where we made Steve Jobs sound like somebody you'd find in a science fiction movie. We want to go through that story and show you how we translated that story into myth, while *still* staying faithful to the facts of Jobs' life. We'll do that by going through the nine stages that we just discussed, so you can see just how well Jobs' life fit this powerful StorySelling™ template:

Stage 1: The Ordinary

Our Story: *Abandoned by his parents at birth, the young hero was raised by a kindly, humble couple in a small village. The father schooled the boy in the ways of alchemy, showing him how to put to work every day earthly forces in combinations that made astonishing things happen.*

The Real Story: Steve Jobs' mother gave him up for adoption – and a couple in the San Francisco area took him in. Jobs had a typical childhood in a middle class suburb; Jobs' adopted father was a mechanic and introduced the boy to rudimentary electronics (which we're calling "alchemy,") giving him the comfort level he needed with technology._

Stage 2: The Calling

Our Story: *The boy was transfixed by his father's talents. And he was further entranced when he met another boy, an aspiring alchemist, whose talents took the art to a whole new level. Together they discussed creating wondrous things. The hero's mind filled with possibilities that the alchemist had never dreamed of – together, they could achieve much.*

The Real Story: Steve Jobs hooked up with fellow student Steve Wozniak in high school and saw that "Woz" had amazing technical abilities; he was already building PC computer boards when it was a relatively new technology. They began to talk about creating a business together.

Stage 3: The Refusal

Our Story: *But the young hero regularly got in trouble. His mind blocked out the conventional teachings of the community and his irreverent attitude towards authority caused him to question the tried and true – the very qualities that fueled his visionary power.*

The Real Story: Jobs had dyslexia – which made school difficult for him. That, in combination with his anti-establishment mindset turned him against the "normal" suburban values. He dropped out of college, determined to find some meaning elsewhere, even if it meant leaving his ambitions behind.

Stage 4: The Intervention

Our Story: *Disillusioned, the hero sought to find higher meaning in distant lands, where he experimented with magic potions that changed his consciousness in profound ways. He further sought the advice and mentorship of gifted mystics who would open up new worlds of thought to the young hero.*

The Real Story: At this point, Steve Jobs went on a seven month retreat to India in search of a Hindu master who, he discovered upon arrival, had recently died. He took several LSD trips there. He also became a practitioner of Zen Buddhism and actually returned with his head shaved, wearing Indian clothing. He later termed this period as one of the most important of his life, because it completely transformed his thought process.

Stage 5: The Beginning

Our Story: *Refreshed and re-energized, he returned to his homeland, determined to discover the destiny that he felt was calling to him – loudly and insistently. He reunited with the alchemist and committed himself to his dreams.*

The Real Story: Jobs returned to the Silicon Valley and worked with Woz at Atari, the video game company. After working on some projects together, they co-founded Apple and built the first Apple computer with an investment by a former Intel manager.

Stage 6: The Challenge

Our Story: *The hero had many early successes – but found it difficult to manage his newfound power. More ominously, the young hero also struggled with the darkness that still lurked in his own consciousness – he found himself at war not only with himself, but with those around him. Still, the hero was besieged with followers who gifted him with riches and accolades. He became the unofficial ruler of the community – and was soon overwhelmed with his new fame and the obligations it entailed.*

The Real Story: Apple began to gather a large cult following, but Jobs' perfectionism and his occasional arrogance alienated a lot of people at the company. His standing in the computer world grew, but he had difficulties balancing his business responsibilities and his single-minded obsession with creating revolutionary products.

Stage 7: The Loss

Our Story: *Desperate for help, the hero took on a clever apprentice, wise to the ways of the world and able to continue to communicate with the hero's followers in his place. The apprentice was untrustworthy, however, and lusted after the hero's power; he turned the hero's followers against him and the hero was exiled from the community he had created. The* *hero, banished to obscurity, was at his low point. His reputation was destroyed and his magic had been stolen.*

The Real Story: Jobs hired PepsiCo Marketing Director John Sculley to be the new CEO of Apple; he would run the business and Jobs could continue to focus on the products. Sculley, however, thought Jobs spent too much money and was too mercurial to be controlled – and convinced the Apple board to fire Jobs from his own company.

Stage 8: Rebirth

Our Story*: And then a strange thing happened. Freed of the pressures of his responsibilities, the hero's spirit grew lighter. He rekindled his youthful passion – and began to work with other alchemists to take his visions to an entirely new level. Meanwhile, the apprentice who had usurped the hero's mystical throne found whatever magic the hero had left behind was weakening. The people turned against him – and he too was banished.*

The Real Story: Jobs founded a new company and began to experiment with new computer technology. He also funded a new start-up to produce new computer-generated animated films – it would later be renamed Pixar. Meanwhile, Apple floundered without Jobs' influence – Sculley was fired and a new CEO was brought in.

Stage 9: The Return

Our Story*: As the hero's followers began to hear whispered tales of the hero's new achievements, they asked him to return to where he belonged – promising to honor him and allow him to continue to pursue his visions there for the rest of his life.*

The hero gladly returned and gifted the people with more magic than they had ever imagined possible. The community was prosperous and fruitful.

The Real Story: Apple bought Jobs' new business and brought him back to the company, eventually making him the CEO. Jobs came up with the iPod, the iPhone and the iPad and turned Apple into the biggest company in the world. Oh, and Pixar also became the most successful studio in the world.

You can see how the Jobs biography fits perfectly into Campbell's "Ultimate Story" structure – you can also see how easily his story can be retold as an ancient myth, just by changing some key words, but leaving the basic ideas intact. And that's the point. The Ultimate Story works for all situations and for every setting and era.

And it can work for *your* story.

Yes, you're not Steve Jobs – none of us are, he was a one-of-a-kind individual—just like you are. But, we do understand that his story is now finished, and yours isn't, since we hope you're still breathing while you're reading this!

That's why, in the next chapter, we're going to give you some "bite-size" versions of The Ultimate Story that you can put to work for you – so you can be the Luke Skywalker or Princess Leia of your Celebrity Brand.

CHAPTER 6

THE FOUR MOST EFFECTIVE STORYSELLING™ PLOTS
Choosing Your Narrative

So this young actor was down to his last dime. Although he had gotten a few decent roles in movies, he still wasn't making the rent. He had hocked his wife's jewelry and even acted in a soft-core porn movie in a desperate attempt to stay afloat while he worked on his career.

But now he had an idea for a movie - a great movie. He was determined to write the screenplay. He knew it would turn things around. First, however, he needed a few bucks. He went out on the street and sold his dog. It was about all he had left and he only got fifty bucks for it.

He returned to his crummy apartment and kept typing for over 24 hours straight – not stopping until he had finished the script. He knew a producing team that liked him and would read it when it was done – so he wanted to waste no time. He hurried over to their offices with the pages.

They read it. And they went crazy over it. They offered him over a hundred thousand dollars for it – more money than he had ever seen in his life.

And he said, "Fine...as long as I play the lead."

The producers looked at him like he was nuts. Was this guy serious? He was a nobody. They couldn't make him the star.

But he wouldn't budge.

Meanwhile, the producers showed the script to a couple of studios to make sure it was commercial. The studios loved it too – and they wanted to make it, as long as an established star played the lead. They passed it around – some of the biggest superstars at the time expressed interest. The producers went back to the actor and said, "Look, Paul Newman wants to be in this thing. We'll up the price. You can be in the next thing you write. But sell *this* one to us now."

The actor, who wasn't quite sure where his next meal was coming from, again refused. Either he played the lead – or he didn't sell.

Finally, the producers backed down. They loved the script too much – and they decided they could make the movie for a low enough budget that they could at least make their money back. They made the deal – the actor starred in the movie – and the film's success took the world by storm.

If you haven't guessed by now, the movie was *Rocky* and the actor was Sylvester Stallone. Tony Robbins, among other motivational speakers, has used this story over and over again to demonstrate the power of positive thinking and why you have to commit yourself to your goals. Stallone's struggle to realize his dreams was an inspiration to everyone who heard it.

Only one problem with all this...*the story is almost completely fabricated.*

When the first "Rocky" film was released way back in 1976,

the above saga of Stallone's difficulties was a major part of the movie's publicity campaign. In every interview regarding the film, Stallone and the producers would dutifully recite it in convincing detail; Rocky, the story of a down and out underdog boxer, was seen as an amazing parallel to Stallone's actual life.

And nobody questioned it – until thirty years later, when Gabe Sumner, then marketing director of United Artists, spilled the beans (and the producers and other studio execs confirmed his story). Stallone, in reality, was a working actor who had never insisted on playing the title part in his screenplay; however, the producers had a deal that allowed them to make any movie with a budget of less than a million dollars, and *Rocky* fit the bill. Why not put the guy in the lead? They had little to lose and couldn't afford a real star.

And, even though they thought the finished film was a knockout, they knew selling *Rocky* to the movie-going public was going to be an uphill battle and that they needed a gimmick. Having Stallone present the film to critics with his own trumped-up story was that gimmick. For that story to work, however, it had to be effective and had to resonate with the audience – which it did, big time. As Sumner said of the effort, "I don't have to tell you how the press feeds on the underdog story…they ate up the idea that this actor loved his work so much…It all became part of the underdog fabric that brought people in. Period. *They just totally bought into it.*"[1] (Italics are ours.)

Now - wouldn't it be great to have people buy into *you* with the same level of enthusiasm? Without you having to make up a story?

It can be done. In this chapter, we're going to look at some specific StorySelling™ plotlines the Italian Stallion's handlers keyed into that made his publicity campaign a champ – and how you can make them work for you.

---

1 Alex Ben Block, "The Untold Story: 'Rocky' Underdog Origin a Studio Myth," *Hollywood Today*, December 20th, 2006

THE GREAT BASIC PLOTS OF LITERATURE

In the last chapter, we explained "The Ultimate Story" – the narrative that all of mankind's major myths, legends and stories follow. Now, as we mentioned then, that narrative is a little too long and complex for most StorySelling™ purposes. That's why we are now going to break down that Ultimate Story into *smaller* plotlines that still have the same kind of primal power in terms of its impact on people – and can also be more easily utilized for Celebrity Branding.

We're going to begin that process by discussing the stories described by author Christopher Booker in his book, *Seven Basic Plots: Why We Tell Stories*. Booker went beyond just myths and analyzed the most memorable literature, as well as movies and TV shows, to uncover the seven plots that were most frequently employed to the greatest success with readers and audiences.

Those seven plots are as follows:

1) Overcoming the Monster
The "Overcoming the Monster" plotline is pretty simple - the hero discovers something evil threatening his homeland and must go out and conquer it. This covers anything from a knight going out to slay a dragon to James Bond going after Goldfinger.

2) Rags to Riches
In the late 19th century, the American writer Horatio Alger made a career out of this plot, with a series of novels about young boys born into poverty and achieving amazing success. It's still a hugely popular storyline in this country, if not THE most popular. Such modern mega-celebrities as Oprah Winfrey remain a source of fascination precisely because of their journey from incredibly humble roots.

3) The Quest
In The Quest, the hero must leave behind everyday life and go out and seek an object, person, location or just some information that's vital to his or his community's future.

The Lord of the Rings trilogy and the Indiana Jones movies both exemplify this time-honored storyline.

4) The Voyage

In "The Voyage," the hero finds himself sent to a magical place, where everyday rules are no longer in play. At first, the trip is fun until something dark makes itself known, which the hero must conquer. In the process, he or she overcomes some internal problem, and then returns home. Prime examples of this plot are *The Wizard of Oz* and *Gulliver's Travels,* and even the children's classic, *Where the Wild Things Are.* More modern examples would be *Inception* and even *The Devil Wears Prada.*

5) Comedy

This is a pretty obvious category. We've all seen enough comedies to know they're usually about situations that are...well, funny; big misunderstandings or people out of their element trying to pull something off they shouldn't try to attempt or pretending to be something they're not. Think of Woody Allen in his early films faking it as a ladies' man, or, more recently, Will Ferrell being the buffoon in any number of scenarios (half of an ice skating team in *Blades of Glory*, an egotistical newscaster in *Anchorman*, etc.).

6) Tragedy

Tragedy, of course, is the other side of comedy - it's all about the unhappy ending and involves very bad things happening to the protagonist, frequently including his or her death. Shakespeare was big on tragedy - *Romeo and Juliet, Hamlet* and *Macbeth* are all plays where pretty much everybody we like dies. These days, movies like *Scarface* and *Goodfellas* serve as our modern-day tragedies.

7) Rebirth

Rebirth is the storyline that snatches triumph from the jaws of the tragic defeat. It's Ebenezer Scrooge buying the Cratchit family a turkey on Christmas morning in *A Christ-*

mas Carol, it's the town of Bedford Falls giving Jimmy Stewart the money he needs at the end of *It's a Wonderful Life*, and of course, in the most epic (and in our opinion the most significant!) of all rebirths, it's Jesus rising up on Easter morning in The Bible. Rebirth is the overcoming of overwhelming negative events or conditions in a way that gives the viewer or reader hope and inspiration.

Now, you may have noticed that we just described *seven* Basic Plots – but the title of this chapter only refers to *four* StorySelling™ Plots. That's because two of these plots don't always work the way we'd like them to for overall StorySelling™ – while two other plots, we believe, should be combined into one.

We'll start with the two plots that don't always work for StorySelling™: *Comedy* and *Tragedy*. When you're done telling your brand story, do you really want to leave your audience laughing at you – or feeling sorry for you? Not really. A personal brand, especially one linked to your business, has to create reasons to buy from you – or, at the very least, motivate someone to want to pursue a professional relationship with you on some level. Neither Comedy nor Tragedy really can accomplish that in a meaningful way.

However, there is no denying that you can use *elements* of these two plots in your branding; we routinely do just that in the branding films we make for our clients. There's nothing wrong with delivering a laugh or a tear *along the way* – it just shouldn't be your end destination.

Similarly, both can be used to burnish an already-existing Celebrity Brand. It's quite all right for Donald Trump to be the center of a Comedy Central Comedy Roast – his brand easily accommodates that. Many a celebrity has also used Tragedy to seize the spotlight – how many *People* magazine cover stories have you seen where a star admits to a drug addiction or discusses a horrifying personal situation "for the first time?" Again, however, these are cases where the Celebrity Brand is already firmly in place and can get a boost from these StorySelling™ detours.

Finally, the two plots that we believe should be combined are The Quest and The Voyage. That's because, again, you must look at the endgame of any StorySelling™ plotline; The Voyage doesn't quite have one, unless it's combined with a Quest. In other words, if your StorySelling™ involves you entering a strange new world, you should be entering that strange new world *for a reason*.

THE FINAL FOUR

Here, then, are what we consider to be the four most effective StorySelling™ Plots:

1) Overcoming the Monster

2) Rags to Riches

3) The Quest

4) Rebirth

Now, let's delve into this Final Four in more detail to show how Stallone capitalized on them - and how you can too.

StorySelling™ Plot #1: Overcoming the Monster

How Stallone used it: In Stallone's StorySelling™ scenario, the monster he overcame was Hollywood itself – the massive entertainment industry was not going to let a virtual unknown star in a film and damage its box office fortunes. He set up a true David vs. Goliath confrontation that he, improbably, won – and which would make the public root for Stallone, just as if he had "gone the distance" in the ring with the heavyweight champion, as his character Rocky did in the movie.

How you can use it: How might this plot pertain to your Celebrity Brand? Simple. There are plenty of "monsters" that your potential clients and customers want to see destroyed - it's just a matter of identifying the ones that fit into your profession or life story. Perhaps you took on the establishment in some significant way to come out on top – for example, if you're a tax lawyer, you may have won a huge case against the IRS' mammoth bureaucracy. Or you're a financial advisor who saw what the crash of 2008 (another "monster") did to innocent people - and you set out to build an investment strategy that safeguards against that happening. There are many ways to go with this plotline that would pay off for any business.

StorySelling™ Plot #2: Rags to Riches

How Stallone used it: It's very easy to see how the manufactured Stallone story keyed into this attractive narrative – the publicity machine portrayed him as being so broke that he had to sell his dog! Not only that, but he was also portrayed as rejecting a six figure payday to hang on to his dream – which made his success story all the more sweet to the audience.

How you can use it: This is perhaps the easiest plot to translate to StorySelling™, since it's such a universal experience. Most entrepreneurs started with virtually nothing and built their businesses from scratch – and they have plenty of stories to illustrate that point. Even if you come from well-off circumstances, you probably still have stories of the difficulties in beginning your business. For example, our Emmy-nominated branded film, "Car Men," spotlighted car dealer Tracy Myers, whose dad owned his car lot before him. If you think there's not much of a Rags-to-Riches quality to that, you're wrong – because his dad made him start at the bottom, washing cars, and work his way up just like any other newbie.

StorySelling™ Plot #3: The Quest

How Stallone used it: Stallone's quest was obvious – he not only wanted to sell his screenplay, he wanted to star in the movie as well. In the StorySelling™ narrative, he was portrayed as facing numerous incredible obstacles in his struggle to succeed at his Quest. When anyone is in pursuit of a dream, and is willing to face all kinds of hardship to reach that goal, we identify with that person and want a happy ending; we root for his or her success.

How you can use it: First ask yourself, did you undergo a quest of your own to find something unique and special to add to your business? We know personal development experts, for example, who promote the fact that they traveled the world to discover the most innovative and effective meditation techniques. If you had to search for the perfect location or the most powerful product or service to sell, or even just to be the best at what you do, that could be your version of The Quest. Understanding what you went through to find what is most vital about what you do also gives an appreciation of that process, as well as an appreciation of the value of your business. That creates a desire in consumers to *buy* this wonderful "something."

StorySelling™ Plot #4: Rebirth

How Stallone used it: The Stallone StorySelling™ effort pictured him as completely "dead" career-wise, after having had roles in several Hollywood movies – he wouldn't sell his script unless he could star in it, so the movie industry was ready to completely turn its back on him, leaving him destitute and without any possibilities for a turnaround. When they finally agreed to his demand, and the movie went on to become an Oscar-winner, you could definitely say Stallone was reborn.

How you can use it: Look no further than the 2012 Super Bowl for a prime example of using the Rebirth paradigm to power up a brand. When Clint Eastwood walked down a dark alley to sell the comeback of Chrysler, it created such a powerful moment that the commercial became an instant political controversy. And it's not the first time Chrysler pulled off the Rebirth trick to great effect - way back in the 1980's, then-CEO Lee Iacocca promoted the brand in commercials after the car company came back from bankruptcy.

Rebirth is an amazing StorySelling™ plot if you've gone through tough times and made it back to success. You can see this plot in the Steve Jobs story we told in the last chapter – when he was fired from his own company, but came back bigger than ever. That kind of triumph inspires people and makes them want to listen to what you have to say. That's why Rebirth is a powerful and potent plot to use for Celebrity Branding, when it fits your circumstances.

As you can see through the Sylvester Stallone example, you can use elements of *all four* of these basic plots in your StorySelling™, in addition to those of Comedy and Tragedy. The main thing to keep in mind is that at least *one* of these four plots should figure prominently in the story you tell – and provide the basic narrative on which you can hang the rest of your branding story. Simplicity is important, which is why we boiled all the plot points of The Ultimate Story down to this quartet.

And, by the way, all four of those plots share an important attribute that we believe is primarily responsible for their effectiveness in StorySelling™: They are all about *the overcoming of obstacles to achieve a rewarding conclusion.* Whether you've overcoming the monster, working out of poverty to achieve wealth, leaping over all the hurdles that stand between you and the object of your Quest, or surviving sudden ruin to regain success, you are always *overcoming.* And you're *always beating the odds.*

And *that act of overcoming* is what makes these four plots so universal and so appealing. Life is a constant battle in many ways, a battle that these four plots represent in different ways. When you're honest about your struggles, your audience relates – and when you triumph over them, your audience stands up and cheers…

…just like at the end of (what else?)…a *Rocky* movie!

CHAPTER 7

YOUR STORYSELLING™ LOGLINE
The First Step to Your Narrative

So the head of the hip, cutting-edge ad agency was stymied. His client was just beginning to turn around his company's staid image – and was counting on the agency's new group of TV spots to complete its return to greatness.

And the head of the agency was very pleased with the work his creative team had done. They had produced six different commercials with six different scenarios, but a common dynamic feel to them. He knew the spots would break through the clutter and deliver the message the company desperately *needed* to deliver.

The only problem was that the agency couldn't think of what *words* to use to deliver that message. It had to be a catchy, simple slogan that brought together all the different commercials with a powerful unifying vision.

But nobody could come up with the words that worked the way he *wanted* them to work. Which meant they didn't really have a finished campaign yet.

Now, it was almost midnight and the agency head was beginning to panic. They had to have the slogan in place tomorrow to show the client. So he paced around at home trying to think of something - *anything* - that might work.

And for some reason Norman Mailer came to mind.

He had recently read Mailer's Pulitzer Prize-winning book, *The Executioner's Song* about the murderer Gary Gilmore, who Mailer had gotten to know when the convict was on death row. And he suddenly remembered what Gilmore's last words were before they flicked on the switch of the electric chair where he was seated.

"Let's do it," Gilmore had said.

The agency head remembered those words and how brave they had seemed to him, even coming from the mouth of a ruthless killer. It was a strong statement. And it seemed to him like it was exactly the kind of statement they needed.

But "Let's" was wrong. Everything wasn't a group activity.

It should be "Just." "Just do it."

He thought that just might work for Nike.

Believe it or not, the above is a totally true story. Dan Wieden, one of the partners in the innovative Wieden Kennedy ad agency (the ad agency's work propelled Nike to be named "Advertiser of the Year" twice at the Cannes Film Festival, the only company ever to have that honor), was completely stuck for a Nike slogan – until he remembered Gary Gilmore's last words.

But that's not how the creation of "Just Do It" was told for about twenty years. For obvious reasons, Wieden and Nike didn't think it was a great idea to make public the fact that Nike's famous slogan was inspired by a cold-blooded murderer. Instead, Wieden just said it came about by accident in a meeting with Phil Knight, the head of Nike – until he finally admitted the truth in a documentary a few years ago.

THE LOWDOWN ON LOGLINES

Wieden had to find a way to verbalize the image he and Nike wanted to project; it certainly wasn't easy, but it proved to be worth the effort. Even though the words came from a very unusual source, "Just Do It," of course, became one of the most well-known advertising slogans of the past few decades.

As you can see, trying to sum up the appeal of a brand can be a very tricky, difficult business; even though you only need to come up with a few words, they have to be the *right* words in order to convey the uniqueness of your brand. But until you're able to do it, it's going to be virtually impossible to use the power of StorySelling™ to your advantage.

In this chapter, we want you to take the first step towards building your StorySelling™ narrative – and that process begins with identifying your StorySelling™ "logline." If you don't know what a logline is, it's a short one-to-three sentence encapsulation of the plot of a movie or TV show that's used to quickly sum it up – a little longer than an advertising tagline like "Let's Do It," but just as vital to defining what your Celebrity Brand is all about.

If you ever visit the movie and television indexing site, IMDB. com, you'll find millions of examples of loglines. Here are a couple of examples:

The CBS comedy *2 Broke Girls*: "Two young women waitressing at a greasy spoon diner strike up an unlikely friendship in the hopes of launching a successful business - if only they can raise the cash."

The Leonardo DiCaprio thriller, *Inception*: "In a world where technology exists to enter the human mind through dream invasion, a highly skilled thief is given a final chance at redemption which involves executing his toughest job to date: Inception."

As you can see in both of the above cases, a logline defines the main character(s), the situation – and the challenge. You need to do something similar with your logline. You'll probably need a few more words than Dan Wieden ended up using, because you're telling more of a story – but again, it still needs to be the *right* story.

THE OBITUARY TEST

So - how do you go about figuring out what the right logline is for your brand?

Don't worry, we're here to help.

We've discovered an incredibly useful exercise that will help you narrow your story down to its most important elements; it was created by author Klaus Fog and it's called "The Obituary Test"[1] (…yes, we know we started this chapter with Gary Gilmore and now we're talking about obituaries, but, believe me, we don't mean to be morbid!).

The Obituary Test is best summed up by the lyrics in Joni Mitchell's classic song, "Big Yellow Taxi" – "You don't know what you've got 'til it's gone." In other words, what would your clients and customers miss the most about you if you were suddenly no longer around? By considering what your absence would mean to the people who buy from you, you can more easily uncover what's important about your story – because you're forced to identify what elements are the most crucial and compelling about your personal brand. This, in turn, helps you immensely in creating your StorySelling™ logline.

The exercise itself is simple – just write your "obituary," as if you were no longer with us (maybe get somebody to send you flowers to put you in the mood). As you do so, keep in mind the following questions:

• What's the biggest thing your business will be
  remembered for?

• What about the way you ran your business will be
  the most missed?

1 Klaus Fog, *Storytelling: Branding in Practice*, (Springer Heidelberg Dordrecht 2010), p. 72

- Which customers will miss you the most and why?

- How were you different from others in the same
  business as you?

Most importantly, be *honest and factual* when you write your obituary – only write what your customers and clients *would actually know and remember* about you. And don't be embarrassed - nobody else has to see it except you (although it would be great if you shared it with people you trust and who know you well, to get their honest reactions).

You should also put some effort into creating the correct *headline* for your obituary – the first thing customers would write about you, based on your professional image. Because *that* is going to be your "Just Do It" moment. So go ahead and write that obituary. We'll wait. Take your time, we'll just check our email and maybe update Facebook…

Okay, all done?

Good. Now….we want you to write that obituary *again*.

Don't groan, this is our own twist on The Obituary Test and we think it's really the key to making it work - because this time, we want you to write your obituary the way YOU would like it to read. In other words, *don't* write it based on how your customers currently perceive you – but, instead, based on how you *want* to be perceived by them.

Let's use some make-believe obituary headlines as an example of what we're talking about. Let's say you're an investment consultant…and maybe, if your obit was printed today, it might read:

LOCAL FINANCIAL PLANNER DIES; SERVED CLIENTS FOR 23 YEARS

But maybe you'd like it to read…

LOCAL FINANCIAL PLANNER SAFEGUARDED AND GREW CLIENTS' FORTUNES FOR DECADES

You can see the difference. The first headline is just a description; the second headline *tells a story*.

Here are a few other examples of obituary headlines that would reflect a lifetime of successful StorySelling™:

CEO BATTLED CHILDHOOD POVERTY TO BUILD SUCCESSFUL BUSINESS

INTERNET MARKETER MADE CLIENTS INTO MILLIONAIRES

INNOVATIVE DENTIST USED CUTTING-EDGE TECHNOLOGY TO HELP PATIENTS

REAL ESTATE AGENT'S CHARITY WORK BONDED HER TO COMMUNITY AND CLIENTS

You see what we mean? These headlines differentiate their subjects and make them *more* than just another professional. They're known for something *specific* and *beneficial* that they accomplish. So go ahead. Work on that second obituary. It's okay, we'll go return a few phone calls…

Finished with the second one? Awesome. Now, take a look at the first one you wrote and compare it with your second one. If they're pretty similar, you're in good shape; if they're very different, however, you're looking at the distance that StorySelling™ will need to transport your Celebrity Brand. You want to get it to a place where that *second* obituary is the default perception customers have about you; it's that perception that will not only bond them more strongly to you or your company, but also attract a multitude of new clients on a consistent basis.

Now, many of you may have had difficulty coming up with that second obit. You weren't sure what to write – or aren't happy with what you ended up writing. Whatever the case is, we assure you, you're not alone; remember Dan Wieden pacing the floor at midnight. So, if you're having trouble coming up with your logline, let's drill a little deeper and see if we strike oil.

LOGLINES OF THE RICH AND FAMOUS

If you are at a loss for words with your logline, your next step should be to review all your options so you can "shop and compare." Then you can more easily make a final decision on what elements you want to use.

Remember, whatever your logline ends up being, it will need to have in place the following four elements (discussed at length in Chapter 4) in order to be effective:

1) Simplicity

2) Authenticity

3) Visibility[2]

4) Relevancy

Also remember that your logline should be represented in some way in *almost everything you do moving forward.* Let's talk about two business legends where that's exactly the case - here's how their loglines might read:

Donald Trump: A blunt, straight-talking billionaire, a guy who's the master of the "Art of the Deal," takes on celebrities and politicians alike as he aggressively expands his business brand and empire.

Richard Branson: A brash youthful business mogul who enjoys exploration and extreme sports constantly pushes the envelope with sexy new ventures and exciting new adventures.

We think you'll agree that Trump and Branson's loglines follow them wherever they go and whatever they do; you'd never confuse the two business moguls, that's for sure.

For example, when Donald Trump shows up somewhere, he demands to be the center of attention; he also carries with him the aura of being the savviest and richest guy in the room, and

---

2 Visibility will most likely be something you'll have to create down the line, so don't worry a
  great deal about that at the moment.

he always gives the impression of shooting right from the hip whenever he speaks. Every deal he talks about doing is going to be "huge" and everybody who disagrees with him is a "moron" or an "idiot." It's not the way we do business, but he certainly makes it work for him.

Branson, in contrast, positions himself as the business version of James Bond; as a matter of fact, he arranged to have a cameo appearance in *Casino Royale* by loaning the producers a plane for the movie. He once arrived at a Miami Beach press conference in a speedboat flanked by a couple of bikini-clad beauties and puts a premium on showcasing his involvement in extreme sports and other outdoor adventures. When you think of Branson or his Virgin brand, you think of something that's daring, different and even *fun*.

Both Trump and Branson have successfully merged their personal brands with their professional brands to the point where they are inseparable. That makes them stand out from the herd and attracts investors to their projects and media attention to their every move.

Now – let's help you do the same.

DEVELOPING YOUR LOGLINE

Your logline can focus on one of several different aspects of your personal and professional life, depending on what works best for your Celebrity Brand. In this section, we're going to ask you some questions – six of them to be exact. Your answers will hopefully help you identify the key points that make you stand out – and that will attract others to your story.

• **Question #1: What have you done?**

Personal stories of overcoming hardship and/or outstanding accomplishment are always valuable to a Celebrity Brand.

Fans of the legendary motivational speaker and author Zig Ziglar, who recently passed away, knew and loved his personal story: the 10th of 11 children whose father died when he was six and only realized his potential when a supervisor motivated him to greatness in his salesman job.

Similarly, Dan Kennedy, a direct marketing legend that we'll discuss in greater detail later in this book, has exploited his background as a copywriting genius who took on the advertising establishment with his famous "No B.S." approach. He tells his "herd" that he's the living proof that there's more than one way to sell successfully.

And, by the way, some people use elements of their backgrounds that don't really have anything at all to do with their current professions. For example, one of our clients is a real estate investment expert in Canada who used to be a policeman; he now positions himself as "The Wealthy Cop," in spite of the fact that law enforcement has precious little to with buying and selling homes. It doesn't matter though – because people (a) remember who he is because of that nickname and (b) trust him more because he was a policeman.

• **Question #2: Who are you?**

We're looking for more than your name here – we're looking for personal qualities you possess that make you stand out from others *like* you.

Think of President Ronald Reagan's old nickname – "The Great Communicator." His "brand" was his ability to convey complex information in simple terms everyone could understand and relate to. Think of legendary soul singer James Brown's designation as "The Hardest Working Man in Show Business" – meaning you knew that when you went to see his show, you would see a *show*.

So - what about you makes you distinct? And remember, it could be as simple as something you wear (remember Larry King and his suspenders night after night?).

• Question #3: What's your title?

When Michael Jackson was at his peak, MTV desperately wanted to have him on an awards show. He said, "Sure – if you agree to call me 'The King of Pop' every time you refer to me." MTV shrugged and said, "Whatever" – they didn't care, as long as he showed. Result? People began to call him "The King of Pop" everywhere he appeared and that's how he was referred to in the press when he died.

Even though it's a title *he created for himself!*

So, we guess, the real question here shouldn't be "What's your title?" – but, "What do you want your title to be?" If it actually fits your situation, as it did with Jackson, you can make it stick. Another one of our clients, Richard Seppala, helps small companies realize more money from their marketing, so he calls himself "The ROI Guy." That's *his* title and that's how people remember him.

• Question #4: How is your product or service different?

Another compelling logline you may be able to write could have to do with an innovative product or service that sets you apart from the competition. For instance, we know who Colonel Sanders was because his KFC chain used his "top-secret" chicken recipe to StorySell their authenticity and food quality; similarly, entrepreneur Wally Amos used his personality and his delicious cookie recipe to StorySell his "Famous Amos" cookie line (and what's interesting about both men is that they both sold out to other companies, who continued to StorySell them even after they were no longer involved!).

So how is your product or service different? Is it faster (think of the 5 Minute Car Wash)? Is it bigger (Burger King is "Home of the Whopper," after all)? Is it just simply better ("It's not TV. It's HBO.")? If it really stands out, you're the person who *made* it stand out – and that makes you more impressive in your logline.

• Question #5: What's your attitude?

In 1911, Thomas Watson was tired of sitting through uninspiring business meetings – so one day, he just got up, walked over to the easel and wrote the word, "THINK" in big letters on the paper. Three years later, when he started IBM, he remembered that moment and made that word a single word slogan that is still used to represent the business machine giant today (their company magazine is called *Think*).

Almost a century later, when Steve Jobs was ready to take over Apple again in 1997, he wanted a similar impactful statement to define his company – so he launched a multimillion dollar campaign around *two* words: "Think Different." Many saw it as a direct response to IBM's *one* word.

Whatever the case, both men used their basic philosophy – or attitude - as the underpinning for their loglines. Even Nike's modified Gary Gilmore line, "Just Do It," is all about attitude. Maybe your particular approach makes you memorable – if so, tap into it.

• Question #6: What do you promise?

FedEx pledges that they'll deliver to "The World on Time." The U.S. Postal Service, in contrast, says, "If It Fits, It Ships." Meanwhile, UPS insists that nobody's better than them at "Logistics." Three different delivery systems all focusing on different benefits - or *promises*.

Many successful brands and businesses have been built on promises – such as the Domino's Pizza chain, with their guarantee that deliveries would come in "30 Minutes or Less" promise (a promise they had to abandon after too many drivers, desperate to make their deadlines, got into dangerous accidents) and Wal-Mart with "Always Low Prices, Always."

So - what promise can you (or do you) consistently deliver on? Is it strong enough to be a part of your logline?

These are the main crucial areas you can explore to create your own logline. Some of these areas overlap and you may end up tapping into more than one of them for your final composition (as long as you keep it simple!).

Now, only you can decide what is the right logline for your StorySelling™ narrative. Again, however, it's useful to do a reality check by showing your choice to friends and associates, as well as any branding consultants you might employ, to ensure your logline is both authentic and impactful. Remember - just because it works for you doesn't necessarily mean it will work for your customers, so feedback is essential.

Once you've decided on your logline, consider it the foundation of your StorySelling™ efforts; from here, you'll build an overall narrative that strengthens your Celebrity Brand and allows you to create powerful extensions of that brand that will carry through into everything you do on a professional – and sometimes, personal – level (just as Trump's and Branson's brands do).

In the next chapter, we'll explore how you put together that narrative. And don't worry, it won't end up being your obituary – it'll be more like your Celebrity Branding® birth announcement!

CHAPTER 8

THE STORYTELLING BEHIND STORYSELLING™
Six Marvelous Steps to Implementing Your Narrative

So Stanley Lieber, at the age of 17, had no idea what to do with his life. Fortunately, however, he could at least earn a paycheck, thanks to the time-honored practice of nepotism. His uncle owned a comic book company and installed the young man in the offices as an assistant in 1939. Stanley saw it as just a temporary situation; he knew that one day he would write the Great American Novel,

A couple of decades later, he was running the place – only there wasn't much left to run. A crackdown on bloody horror comics in the 1950's had caused many organizations and parents to ban them altogether – and the ones that had survived were so heavily censored that they didn't generate many sales on their own. In the glory days of comics, Stanley had been supervising over twenty people – now he was down to having only three or four staffers working fulltime for him, grinding out stories about monsters from outer space for the boys - and harmless teen romances for the girls.

But DC Comics, the perennial industry leader, had just had some success with a new superhero group title, The Justice League of America, which brought together Batman, Superman and a bunch of other costumed crusaders – so Stanley's uncle suggested that he create one as well. Stanley wasn't happy with the whole idea. As a matter of fact, he was ready to quit the whole business. Superheroes were kind of silly and they had been out of fashion for years. He didn't want to write another copycat comic: he was convinced he needed a career change if he was ever really going to make his creative mark.

So he went home and talked through his frustrations with his wife. She was frustrated with those frustrations and finally told him, "Look, don't just quit. You've been going through the motions for years, doing what everybody else was telling you to do. Do this one the way you want to do it, put everything into this new comic and see what happens. You can always quit later."

Stanley thought about it and finally decided, why not? He didn't have anything to lose – he might as well go for it. So, using his pen name of Stan Lee, he created *The Fantastic Four* with artist Jack Kirby - and was as shocked as anybody when the sales figures came in a few months later; kids were buying up the new comic like crazy. His uncle, always ready to drive whatever was successful into the ground, quickly ordered him to make more superhero comics, so Stan did. In short order came an incredible creative burst that produced *Spider-Man*, *The Incredible Hulk*, *The X-Men*, *Iron Man*, *The Mighty Thor* and *The Avengers* – it was like something inside Stanley had been finally unleashed.

And that something began to find its way into every part of the business. Stan rebranded the whole line, calling it "Marvel Comics," and gave every cover the same distinctive design. He pushed the boundaries of traditional comics publishing and storytelling in every way; in-jokes abounded, and adventures were continued from issue to issue for the first time, just like soap operas. Stories were also more adult; they were an entirely new combination of the boy-girl dramas Stan had concocted for his romance comics, traditional superhero sagas and, for the first time, an irreverent humor that permeated almost every page.

The world at large took notice of the big Marvel movement. Soon respectable magazines like *Esquire* and *Rolling Stone* were publishing serious profiles of Stan and Marvel. Their readership now didn't stop when kids turned twelve; college kids were reading his stuff and loving it.

Stan "the Man" Lee suddenly found that he had become a comics legend by creating an entirely new narrative for the industry. By the mid-70's, he had made his mark and, finally, was ready to move on. And he did – to Hollywood.

It took Stan Lee another couple of decades to find big success in superhero movies, but *The Avengers* was crowned the box office champion of 2012 – as the popularity of all the Marvel characters Stan Lee created fifty years ago hit its all-time high, mostly because many of the StorySelling™ techniques Lee used in the comics were finally applied to the film adaptations.

Stan Lee created a logline for himself and Marvel that shattered the comics' stereotype and produced a hip, fun and smart image that was personality-driven and fit perfectly with the growing youth movement of the 60's. More importantly, he took that logline and applied it to *every aspect of the Marvel business* – creating a money-making mythology that culminated recently with the Disney Corporation purchasing the company for *four billion dollars.*

That's the power of StorySelling™.

In this chapter, we're going to analyze the "Marvelous Steps" that Stan Lee took to implement the StorySelling™ concepts we've talked about in this book – and you'll see for yourself how those concepts can be applied in *a practical* way in a business to spur incredible success. We'll also offer the questions you need to ask yourself in order to successfully implement Stan's incredibly effective Marvelous Steps into your own Celebrity Brand.

THE LOGLINE THAT CHANGED A BUSINESS

Before we get into those Marvelous Steps, however, we want to point out something that's relevant to what we've discussed in the last three chapters. You may have read those chapters and thought, "I don't get what plots and narratives have to do with anything. How does this help me grow a business?"

Well, let's dig deeper into how it helped Stan Lee grow an *empire,* let alone a business.

Here's the challenge he faced when he was told to create a new superhero comic in 1961: At the time, DC Comics, home of Superman and Batman, was like Ford, General Motors and Chrysler combined when it came to the comics business – they were the "gold standard" and completely dominated it. Stan Lee's comic company, in contrast, was a shrinking, struggling business that had no identity – and seemingly no future.

Now, here's what's *really* interesting about Stan's story; the idea to create a new superhero comic wasn't his, it was his boss's. And the idea to create a new *kind* of superhero comic wasn't his, it was his wife's.

What was his idea? The *StorySelling*™.

If we were to actually put down on paper the logline he had in his head, it would be worded like this: "An upstart with no money and few resources challenges the world's biggest comic company on their own turf. Through humor, intelligence and innovation, that upstart creates an entirely *new* approach to comics that brings in a whole new audience."

Remember our four most effective StorySelling™ plots from Chapter 6?

1) Overcoming the Monster

2) Rags to Riches

3) The Quest

4) Rebirth

All FOUR are contained in that logline. DC Comics was the "Monster" that had to be overcome, Marvel quickly went from "Rags to Riches," "The Quest" was Stan Lee's journey to find a new way of doing comic books that would give him some career satisfaction and "Rebirth"…well, Stan Lee and Marvel both experienced that after both almost went out of business.

So, practically speaking, you can see how those four plotlines are directly responsible for a great deal of Marvel's successful StorySelling™. Now, we're certainly not saying Stan ever consciously articulated any of this – for him, it was a simple matter of doing things the way *he* wanted to do things. But, being a natural-born storyteller *and* promoter (the combination is crucial), he instinctively understood how to put these principles into action, so he could stop blindly *reacting* to the competition and create his own narrative – which is precisely what StorySelling™ is all about.

And comic book readers dug that story; he and Marvel became *authentic* in a way he had never been before and suddenly, next to Spider-Man and Iron Man, Superman and Batman looked like the squarest dudes in town.

And is that any different than what Apple did to Microsoft? Nope.

As we've been saying throughout this book, StorySelling™ sets you apart from the competition. And, if your narrative has the right StorySelling™ elements, it attracts new customers and helps you keep old ones.

But you must make your StorySelling™ a part of *every* aspect of your business approach in surprising and interesting ways that will continue to make your audience want to see what happens next (just like any good story). Crafting your logline is a great start – but, in this chapter, we want you to think about the next important steps involved in implementing and integrating your

StorySelling™ throughout your business model.

With that in mind, let's examine a few steps Stan took to make his StorySelling™ a vital part of the Marvel mythos from top to bottom - and how you should think about doing the same for yourself.

MARVELOUS STEP #1: START SUBTLE

Stan Lee never came out and said he was going to change the face of comic books. Instead, he quietly took his wife's advice and created a new kind of superhero group – one that had human flaws, internal conflicts and adult attitudes. In other words, he let the work itself do the talking and attract the attention.

When you begin your StorySelling™ efforts, concentrate on bringing your logline to life in your actual Celebrity Brand – or your product or service - before you make claims you might not deliver on. When you see something is starting to work, you can then exploit that successful narrative. The Hall of Failures is littered with overhyped products that fell with a thud heard around the world when they didn't live up to the expectations created by their parent company (The infamous Ford Edsel, "New Coke," Microsoft's Zune line of media players, etc.) – don't hype unless you're sure you've got the back-up to prove it.

Implement this Step by Asking Yourself: What "proof" can I generate of my own expertise or product/service superiority? Will it take the form of outstanding performance, believable testimonials, branded books or videos, or simply product popularity?

MARVELOUS STEP #2: BE BOLD WHEN IT'S TIME

Stan didn't know he had a hit on his hands until he was ready to go to press with the third issue of *The Fantastic Four*. At that point, he decided it was time to go full throttle – and he boldly put across the top of the comic cover, "The World's Greatest Comic Magazine," a claim that continued to stay put for decades. Similarly, Steve Jobs, *after* Apple had attracted a devoted group of customers, spent a record-breaking amount of money on a commercial entitled *1984* that ran only one time during the Super Bowl of that same year to make his own monster StorySelling™ statement.

When you've got proof of your greatness, go with it. Until then, wait it out until your StorySelling™ is recognized in one way or another.

Implement this Step by Asking Yourself: *How can I best exploit my proof? What's the most memorable way to promote this fact that's consistent with my StorySelling™ narrative – and appropriate to my audience?*

MARVELOUS STEP #3: STORYSELL EVERYWHERE

Just like a great cook can make dishes from virtually every part of an animal, Stan Lee decided to look for StorySelling™ possibilities in every inch of his comic books – even the features into which publishers rarely put any thought or energy. Stan gave the letters pages hilarious names (Iron Man's was *Sock It to Shellhead*), he filled a page in each comic with what he called *Bullpen Bulletins*, spotlighting and cross-promoting other Marvel comics, and he started a wacky fan club, The Merry Marvel Marching Society (or MMMS, for short), that was a huge success. He took what other comic books saw as *obligations* and approached them as *opportunities* – another way Marvel stood out from the rest was to create an incredible bond between it and its readers.

Implement this Step by Asking Yourself: *What overlooked opportunities are there in my industry that I can use for StorySelling™ purposes? How can I insert my narrative into those areas in a creative and impactful way?*

MARVELOUS STEP #4: DON'T FORGET THE FACES

There was something else Stan Lee did that was unprecedented in his industry – he began to give the artists and other writers (and even the guys who lettered the word balloons!) funny nicknames in the story credits – in a business where nobody had even *put* credits on stories before. Not only that, but he frequently talked about them in the Marvel Bullpen Bulletins and even recorded a wacky comedy record with them that was sent to all members of the MMMS.

Result? The men and women *behind* Marvel Comics became almost as important as the superheroes were to the readership, creating an even stronger bond to it. Stan, of course, put himself the furthest out front, with his own regular column in the *Bullpen Bulletins* and regularly commenting on his own stories with goofy footnotes that either admitted story mistakes or explained something that had happened in another comic book.

The lesson? Always make sure to have some kind of strong personality involved with your StorySelling™ efforts, whether it's you, someone who works for you or even a hired spokesperson; people identify, of course, with people and create the emotional involvement you want to create with your narrative.

Implement this Step by Asking Yourself: Who will be the face (or faces) of my StorySelling™? How does the chosen personality (or personalities) fit into my narrative?

MARVELOUS STEP #5: ALWAYS ENGAGE

You'll note a very strong element to everything Stan Lee did that we've discussed so far – he *engaged* comic book readers on a level than had never happened before. Through his wacky letter pages, Bullpen Bulletins, credits, story footnotes and fan club, *he was constantly talking directly to his readers in an entertaining way.* And he found unique ways to turn even negatives into positives with this attitude. For instance, the Marvel Universe grew so complicated that readers began writing in to complain when a story got something wrong or contradicted an earlier story. This was a growing problem – so Stan decided that every reader who correctly identified a mistake would win a "No-Prize." What was a No-Prize? Well, the winner would receive an envelope in the mail with a big announcement printed on it that their No-Prize was inside.

What was in the envelope? Nothing.

Implement this Step by Asking Yourself: What opportunities do I have to engage in a new and unique way with my customers? How can I make that engagement as memorable as possible?

MARVELOUS STEP #6: CONTINUE TO EVOLVE

One thing we should make clear is that Stan Lee didn't do all of the great StorySelling™ feats we're describing in this chapter all at once. Instead, they evolved in a very organic way over time (but in a pretty short period of time, all things considered), as he obviously kept spotting new things to do with the comic book format as his StorySelling™ efforts continued to gain traction.

He also deepened the Marvel narrative as it progressed. As more and more readers regarded Marvel as the cool "alternative" to DC, Stan made more and more fun of DC in his editorial content to reinforce that positioning and to reflect Marvel's growing success.

That growth occurred in the actual comics' content as well. In the late '60's, Marvel became the first major comic book company to break the Comics Code Authority's long list of rules (the Code had been instituted in the 50's to self-police comics and reassure parents). The Code had it that you couldn't portray drug use in any comic story – but, as addiction was becoming a serious problem with teens in the late 60's, the only way Stan Lee could take on the problem in *Spider-Man* was disregarding the Code – so he did, and created a very memorable, talked-about series of issues.

Implement this Step by Asking Yourself: Is my StorySelling™ keeping pace with what's happening with my business? Am I reflecting the present – or only the past?

Stan Lee's big mistake during his first twenty years in the comic book business was seeing it as a job and not an opportunity. Most of you reading this book have probably made that same mistake at one time or another – it's the difference between an employee and an entrepreneur. When he finally saw that he had the power to make something completely new happen with his comics, he used that power – and found out that it packed a lot more punch than any that The Hulk ever threw.

When you develop a strong StorySelling™ narrative and implement it correctly, as Stan did, it feeds on itself, it grows stronger and stronger, and it opens up more and more layers of opportunity as you move forward with it. There were very few businesses in 1961 sillier, more inconsequential and perceived to have less of a future than comic books – and yet Stanley Lieber took that business and transformed it in such a dynamic way through StorySelling™ that, a half-century later, it's paying its biggest dividends ever – both for himself and the company.

And for that, we salute Stan with the one word he uses as a sign-off in whatever he writes: "Excelsior!"

CHAPTER 9

PUTTING YOUR STORYSELLING™ ALL TOGETHER
The Branded Film

He always had a big mouth. And it was always getting him in trouble.

And he certainly wasn't good at dealing with authority – that was one of the big reasons he dropped out of college during his freshman year. Another reason was he wanted to start his own underground newspaper at the age of eighteen – it was the sixties and he had a lot to say.

Eventually, he built the paper up into a statewide success – and a national magazine came knocking on his door. He was ready for the big time and quickly grabbed the opportunity. Again, he made his presence known – and became one of the star writers at the magazine: So much of a star, that, after a few years, he was promoted to editor.

He was running the whole show now and he didn't intend to back down about anything – which the publishers, much to their displeasure, discovered when he refused to run an article they were adamant about putting in the next issue. He said it was inaccurate and overblown. They said...he was fired.

He had been editor for less than a year.

Never one to take things sitting down, he sued for wrongful termination and settled the suit out of court for $58,000.

But what was he going to do now? He was thirty-four years old and unemployed - with a reputation for being difficult. He knew he would quickly burn through the money if he didn't do something to get himself back into the spotlight quickly.

So...with the settlement money, he decided to make a movie about his hometown and the economic difficulties it was having in the late 1980's recession. But he wanted to make what he called an "anti-documentary" – something that was entertaining and fun to watch. And, since the movie needed someone on-camera to place in some outrageous situations he was planning to create, he hired himself – because he couldn't afford anyone else.

In 1989, Michael Moore finished *Roger and Me* – and it instantly became a critically acclaimed financial success. And because Moore's face was all over the film, *he* instantly became a celebrity – and parlayed his newfound fame into more movies, a TV series, books, an Oscar win and a multi-million dollar career.

And it all started with a Branded Film.

THE POWER OF THE BRANDED FILM

Whether you're for Michael Moore or against him, we'd like you to look beyond his politics for the purposes of this book, and, instead, focus on just how a Branded Film jumpstarted his international success.

Now, if he hadn't been fired from his job at the left-wing publication, *Mother Jones,* he might have ended up making his name as a journalist who maybe got a few TV slots as a pundit on one of the cable news networks. Clearly, however, no one would have offered him rich movie and book deals on the basis of just that.

Instead, he created a memorable logline – "A fat unkempt working class guy from Michigan takes on corporate America all by himself and provokes outrageous confrontations, while proving his political points" – and brought it to life in a compelling narrative. And he did a magnificent job of StorySelling™ himself to liberal Hollywood and sympathetic moviegoers across the country.

The fact is there is no better way to StorySell than with a properly-produced Branded Film – because there's no better way to tell a *story* than with a film. You can actually bring your logline and whatever narrative you choose to life – and show your customers who you are and what you're all about in a persuasive and dramatic fashion.

Morgan Spurlock is another documentary filmmaker who makes sure to insert himself into his films, such as *Supersize Me* and *The Greatest Movie Ever Sold* (which was, ironically, a movie about product placement). This method has made him into a celebrity just as it did for Moore; Spurlock is able to host his own TV shows and is more able to obtain financing for other projects.

And you don't have to make a documentary filmmaker to make this work for you. Anybody remember the inspirational sports movie, *Rudy,* about a 5' 6" kid with bad grades who worked his butt off to get into Notre Dame and into one of their games? Well, the guy who made his dream come true, Rudy Ruettiger, ended up working in a boring insurance company job after that moment of glory – but became obsessed with finding a way to make Hollywood turn his college triumph into a feature film. Ten years later, he somehow made it happen – and, after the movie was released in 1993, he got a call from a motivational speaking bureau and began a whole new career, earning tens of thousands of dollars to tell his story to adoring crowds.

It took a Branded Film to make that happen.

And, by the way, Hollywood even produces Branded films for its *own* projects. When you see one of those "First Look" featurettes on HBO about an upcoming release, you're looking at a Branded Film *about* a film. These shorts are done documentary-style - but they're anything *but* real documentaries: They're actually advertisements produced to *look* like the real story behind the movie - but, of course, you'll never see any material that might be interpreted as being negative. They don't have to put any in – and neither do you.

WHY BRANDED FILMS WORK

There are many reasons Branded Films are essential to creating a powerful Celebrity Brand - here are a few of them:

• *Films Make Stars*
   ...and isn't that just what you want out of your Celebrity Brand?

   In the early days of Hollywood, there was no "star system." Actors were not credited and no one thought twice about what actor to put in a film. It was the *audience* that created movie stars - by demanding more movies featuring performers they saw and liked in different films. Producers finally figured out it was worth it to pay these performers a premium in exchange for the increased audiences they brought in to see them.

   In a Branded Film, you are the "star" - the central figure in your own story, who is presented as a likeable and magnetic individual. The audience responds to you on a gut level that just can't happen with the printed word. If Michael Moore hadn't put himself in his own movie, he never would have had the career clout he enjoyed after the fact.

• *Films Tell Stories*
   When the narrative behind your StorySelling™ is actually

brought to life in a Branded Film, people take it in on a very deep level – and they *remember* it. Why? Because you're able to do your StorySelling™ in the most compelling and dramatic way.

In any action movie, Western, romantic comedy or other popular film genre, various time-tested film techniques - such as how you use editing, music, lighting and camera angles to create moods and effects - are put to work in order to make the story as exciting and suspenseful as possible. An effective Branded Film uses those same sophisticated techniques - and combines them with real people and real locations to give your narrative an authentic power that a Hollywood film can't match. Just ask Michael Moore – the only movie he made with actors and a concocted story (*Canadian Bacon*) bombed badly at the box office.

• *Films Control the Message*
The long-running CBS news series *60 Minutes* built its reputation initially by "ambush" interviews. The reporter would show up, without warning, at the office of the person they were investigating and ask very confrontational questions. That person had no control of the message. If he answered honestly, he might incriminate himself. If he didn't answer at all, he risked looking incredibly guilty.

A Branded Film should be as opposite as you can get from this nightmarish scenario. Interviews and location shooting must be highly planned and scheduled, and the interview questions designed to shape the proper StorySelling™ narrative. It's one of the secrets of Michael Moore's success, by the way – he's been called out repeatedly for deceptive editing and shading reality to make the StorySelling™ in his films more pointed and dramatic.

• *Films Allow People to Know Who You Are*
In a book, you can write that someone's attractive. In a film, you can *see* that a person is attractive. The difference is cru-

cial - in the first instance, someone is telling you something that you have to accept as being true, in the second instance, *you see it for yourself.*

Books are great at conveying ideas and demonstrating your expertise on a subject; they are essential to personal branding. Films do something else entirely - they allow your audience to experience *who you are* - how you walk, talk and look - and respond to you in a *personal* way. Again, Michael Moore's signature appearance, in his baseball cap, jeans and sneakers, resonated with his audience in a way that wouldn't have come across in a picture on a book jacket.

- ### There's Never Been a Better Time to Make One
  A Branded Film is a relatively new arrow in the marketing quiver of entrepreneurs and business owners, for two key reasons, both having to do with technological advances.

Reason number one: Creating and editing high quality films has become much more *affordable* in recent years. You no longer need millions of dollars to create a professional Hollywood-level production. Equipment is much cheaper, more people have access to train on that equipment, and post production can be accomplished on computers not that much more powerful (or expensive) than your average home or office PC.

Reason number two: Online video has exploded on the internet, becoming much more prevalent and powerful. That means a branded film can be shared not only through YouTube.com, but also through popular social media sites such as Facebook and LinkedIn.

Of course, for Celebrity Branding to really be effective, you need to stand out from the herd. Most Branded Films fall far short of the mark in this regard. Even though there are an incredible amount of videos and films being posted to the internet, most of the ones that attempt branding do it in the most basic way possible; the person merely speaks to the camera and explains who they are or what they do. This is effective as a quick introduction to a website, or explaining a specific product or service, but, as far as StorySelling™ a brand goes, it only can do so much – especially if it ends up looking more like a hostage video than a real *movie*.

A successful Branded Film, in contrast, boasts high production values and an impactful emotional story. It raises the bar for the entrepreneur who really wants to present the most polished and professional brand possible, while, at the same time, make the strongest possible emotional connection to both customers and non-customers.

This is just the route the Justin Bieber management team took to boost their client's already red-hot profile when they released the Bieber documentary, *Never Say Never*, to theatres in 2011. This was the ultimate Branded Film event - and was a giant financial success as well, grossing over 70 million dollars in the U.S. alone. As *Forbes* put it, *"Never Say Never* was a brilliant way for the Bieber brand team to tell its story and, just as brilliantly, get it out there when the media wind was at its back. When you're on a roll, do what you can to keep the momentum going."[1]

Of course, when you go to the time, trouble and expense to produce a high-level Branded Film, you want to make sure you have an effective marketing plan in place in terms of how you present that film to your audience. In our next chapter, we'll show you one that worked like gangbusters for one of our clients.

PIXAR'S STORYSELLING™ SECRETS

As we've noted repeatedly, the most important facet to a Branded Film is the *story* you decide to tell. Storytelling is an art – so we thought we'd close this chapter with some winning advice from people who are today's leading practitioners of it. We're talking

---

[1] Allen Adamson, "The Secret Behind Justin Bieber's Brand Success," February 25th, 2011, *Forbes Magazine*

about another friend of Disney, Pixar, the most successful movie studio of all time, with thirteen feature films to its credit that have grossed over seven billion dollars worldwide as of this writing.

Pixar, originally funded by Steve Jobs, has enjoyed an unprecedented combination of artistic and commercial success – nobody else has ever put out that many films in a row without a flop. Probably the biggest reason for that success is that *they always put story first.* They're famous – and sometimes infamous – for getting halfway through production on one of their movies, then deciding the story isn't working and restarting the whole process. Yes, it's an expensive way to work – but their track record argues that it's worth every penny.

Recently, one of Pixar's storyboard artists, Emma Coats, shared many of the guidelines the company uses for their storytelling process. We'd like to thank Ms. Coats for giving us this inside look – and we're also going to borrow a few of them for this chapter, to inspire you to fully develop *your* Branded Film narrative.

**Pixar Story Point #1: Once upon a time, there was _____.
Everyday, _____. One day, _____.
Because of that, _____. Because of that, _____.
Until finally, _____.**

No, this isn't Pixar's version of Mad-Libs; filling in these blanks allows you to flesh out the backbone of any story. When you're constructing your narrative for your Branded Film, you want to make sure the story keeps moving forward – and has a beginning, middle and end. If you watch Michael Moore's first movie, Roger *and Me,* you'll see his attempts to personally confront the head of GM becomes the running narrative – you are hooked because you want to see if he's ever able to pull it off. Part of the criticism surrounding this film is that Moore rearranged the chronology of events – that, in fact, the meeting with Roger Smith happened before other incidents in the film - but he did make that choice to make sure his StorySelling™ worked to the maximum effect.

Pixar Story Point #2: Keep in mind what's interesting to your audience, not to you.

Let's face it – human beings are a self-centered bunch. And sometimes it's hard to get out of our own heads. In a Branded Film, you want to avoid spending too much time on stuff *you* care about, when the people you want to reach probably *don't*. That can actually turn a potentially disastrous corner; we've all seen celebrities go on and on about subject matter that not only doesn't appeal to their fans, but also might just actually offend them. (Anybody remember Tom Cruise lecturing Matt Lauer about psychiatry a few years ago? Or Jenny McCarthy trying to convince everyone that vaccinations cause autism?)

Outside interests and hobbies make you relatable and interesting, but you can't forget your main "logline" when it comes to your StorySelling™. To return to Mr. Tom Cruise, everyone knows he's a Scientologist, but he knows that talking too much about his controversial religion is going to turn people away. However, he had to learn that lesson the hard way after alienating a lot of fans.

Pixar Story Point #3: You admire a character more for trying than succeeding

We all fail in our personal and professional lives at one point or another. We don't like for it to happen, but it's a part of life – it can't be helped and, many would say, it's actually *good* for us; it helps us to learn and grow. But because we all do fail, it's incredibly relatable – and an integral part of Joseph Campbell's Ultimate Story as well as the four plotlines we discussed in Chapter 6. So don't shy away from past mistakes within your Branded Film, as long as you come out a winner at the end.

Pixar Story Point #4: Give your characters opinions.

Pixar adds to the above guideline, *"Passive and malleable might seem likeable to you, but it's poison to an audience."* In other words, if you don't stand for anything, you don't mean anything. Consider how many handsome, smiling leading men pop up in movies and TV shows and quickly disappear – only to be re-placed with a new wave of handsome, smiling leading men. It's more than okay to have a point of view in a Branded Film – as a matter of fact, it's a must; otherwise nothing about you will be all that memorable. People like Michael Moore and Morgan Spur-lock have an appeal to their audiences because they do have a specific perspective within their StorySelling™. Obviously, you don't want to offend half of the people watching your Branded Film, as Moore's movies often do – but you can undoubtedly find one that works for you and appeals to your customers.

Pixar Story Point #5: What are the stakes? Give us reason to root.

As all of the plotlines we've discussed make clear, audiences get more invested in a story when there are big challenges that must be overcome. What are the challenges you can portray in your Branded Film? They could be in your personal story or they could be an integral part of your business (for example, an investment counselor trying to protect his clients' savings in a difficult eco-nomic time). StorySelling™ requires some tension – that tension comes from facing obstacles that can seem insurmountable.

Pixar Story Point #6: Get the obvious out of the way—Surprise yourself.

Nobody wants to watch a movie where they can already guess the ending – unless there are enough surprises along the way to make it fun and interesting. It's all too easy to do what's ex-pected in a Branded Film – that's why we always try to come at our subject matter from unexpected directions and you should too. Obviously, most of these kinds of movies end up as suc-cess stories, because you want to StorySell yourself as someone who's good at what he or she is doing. What you do along the way to get to the positive feel-good conclusion, however, should be as unexpected as possible – and reveal things that the audi-ence never saw coming. For example, even though the entire plot of *Roger and Me* was obviously going to culminate in Michael Moore meeting up with the GM CEO, there was enough loopy humor and incisive social commentary along the way to make the trip memorable.

Pixar Story Point #7: Honesty lends credibility

Branded Films succeed not because they're full of the overhype of an infomercial selling some new, crazy, weight-loss system, but because they're fairly low-key and feature *real* people in *real* locations speaking honestly about you, your life and your business. This approach works for any type of business.

But it actually goes beyond that. When you watch a good movie, you become involved in the characters' lives and what's going to happen to them. You root for them to do well and succeed. And you want to see more of them – that's why Hollywood is so big on sequels.

There are a lot of reasons for this; we covered them in our first few chapters on the psychological and historical power of stories. But it comes down to this: by telling your story, especially in a Branded Film where viewers can actually see what you're all about, you and your company become a *shared experience* with the public. They are magnetically drawn into your professional and personal life, they feel like they're a part of your success story – and they want to see you continue to do well.

And that, in turn, makes them *want to do business with you.*

This all happens on a deep psychological level, because a properly produced Branded Film triggers an amazing amount of empathy that draws viewers closer to you and your business. And, again, it doesn't matter what kind of business it is!

For example, on paper, one of the Branded Films we produced, *Car Men*, would seem to be a ridiculous concept; make an emotional, even touching film about an incredibly outrageous car dealer. But you'll find out just how well it worked...

...in the very next chapter!

CHAPTER 10

STORYSELLING™ IN ACTION
The *Car Men* Case Study

So, in the 1930's, Frank Myers opened a small store in East Bend, North Carolina. It turned out to be a lot more than the birth of a business - it was also the birth of a *story*; a story that helped propel his great-grandson, Tracy Myers, to an awesome marketing triumph in 2011 for both himself and his family's car dealership, Frank Myers Auto Maxx.

That narrative was chronicled in an original Branded Film produced by our CelebrityFilms™ division. And Tracy was smart enough to use the StorySelling™ power of that film to leverage both the local media as well as online social media to make the biggest possible splash in the Winston-Salem area.

From online teases to press releases, from the black-tie premiere at a movie theatre to the DVD release, Tracy brewed the perfect blend of honest hype and hard content to pump up his customer base about the forthcoming film and keep them excited about this unique hometown story told with a Hollywood-style sparkle. But, with apologies to Tracy, the real star of this show was *StorySelling™*.

SUSTAINING YOUR STORYSELLING™

The real point of this chapter is that the StorySelling™ shouldn't stop with the production of your Branded Film. It shouldn't be dumped on the Internet as an afterthought with maybe a few social media links to its YouTube page; that's a gigantic waste.

Instead, your Branded Film should be spotlighted in an exciting "premiere" event that fully exploits its marketing power and takes advantage of its top-level production values. Again, the Branded Film is still a unique commodity in marketing circles - and publicizing it allows you to strongly differentiate yourself from the competition in the public's mind.

For example, when Barack Obama was about to face down John McCain on Election Day in 2008, he used a Branded Film event to push him over the top. A week before the election, his campaign team bought a half-hour of time on three major networks - Fox, CBS and NBC - as well as four smaller channels - all at the same time. Suddenly, a half-hour infomercial was perceived as a multi-channel event, and ended up with a total viewership of over 25 million. In contrast, only 19.8 million viewers had watched the final game of the World Series that year.

THE BIRTH OF *CAR MEN*

As *Car Men* was one of our first Branded Films, we want to provide a little background as to how we came to produce it.

Tracy had been working with us for a few years as a client of our Celebrity Branding Agency®. His accomplishments with his dealership, Frank Myers Auto Maxx, had been (and continue to be) incredibly impressive - he was the youngest person to ever win the Quality Dealer of the Year Award, which marked him as the best used car dealer in the entire country. We helped him expand his universe by making him a, Best-Selling Author, as well as placing him on TV shows on NBC, CBS, ABC and FOX affiliates around the country. He's also been involved in our mastermind groups, been a part of our Best-Seller Summit and is a part of our annual trips to the Grammy Awards in Los Angeles. If you ever visit his Facebook page or website, you'll quickly see that Tracy is a master promoter and marketer.

That's why he was a natural choice when we decided to approach someone about creating a Branded Film – we wanted to prove our theory about how much it could do for a Celebrity Brand. And we were gratified that Tracy instinctively understood what the right film would mean to both himself as well as his business.

Tracy: It was a fairly easy decision, because we'd been looking for a way for many years to be able to separate ourselves from the competition, to where we're not just in the commodities business - which is what selling used cars, trucks, and vans becomes if we're not very careful. When we compete just on price and there's no story, no emotion, no feeling behind what we do, then everyone's going to lose, especially us. So we've been looking for a way to tell our story and get it out in a quality, professional way.... I knew right away that this was perfect.

More importantly, Tracy didn't waste any time latching on to the marketing possibilities of his Branded Film. *Within two days* of his decision to go ahead with it, he put out the public word about the project in the form of a social media status update which read:

"Hey, had a great meeting today. Talked with an award-winning movie maker about the possibility of making a film or documentary here at the dealership. Hopefully big news to follow."

Tracy started a lot of buzz with those three simple sentences

- and his many social media followers and subscribers immediately responded that he should keep them all in the loop and that this was an amazingly cool possibility.

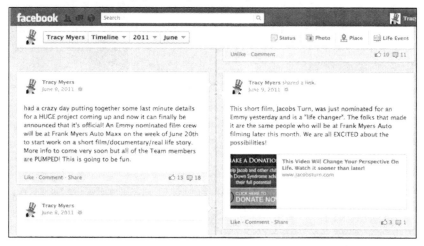

After a few more social media teases, Tracy finally put out the first press release, with the headline, "Owner of Frank Myers Auto Maxx Tapped as Feature Film Subject." But *before* he put it out, he made sure to bump up the buzz an extra notch by calling up all his media connections and giving them a heads-up that something big might be in the wind.

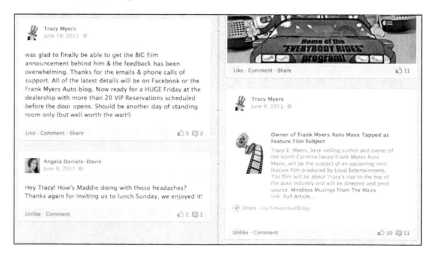

CRAFTING THE *CAR MEN* STORY

As Tracy was busy stoking the sizzle, we had to make sure that there was actually some steak to go along with it. The next phase was zeroing in on what story to tell in the film. As we noted, the Myers family had been business owners in the community for over 80 years - and that seemed to be the most interesting and engaging angle to explore in the movie.

And it truly was. Tracy's dad had been a born salesman and did really well in the car business. Now came the interesting part: even though Tracy grew up around that dealership, he didn't really want to be a part of it. He went to college and focused his studies on his ambition to become a radio disc jockey. He also played with a couple of bands. To make money, however, he began selling used cars at night - out of town at college, so his dad had no idea. Finally, Tracy decided to come back to the family business, but his dad didn't automatically put him on the sales floor. Nope, Tracy had to start from the bottom up - in the wash pit.

Automatically, we had a great StorySelling™ scenario.

Eventually, of course, Tracy did advance and finally took over the dealership. And that's when he put his love of theatrics and the media to work - promoting himself and his dealership with outrageous methods that continue to draw not only attention, but also customers. The other dealers thought he was crazy, but, eventually, they ended up emulating his business model. And, as we mentioned earlier, he ended up being named the best used car dealer in all of America. It's a great story, filled with emotion, conflict and a happy ending.

We knew we had the makings of a great documentary - and, more importantly, a great Branded Film for Tracy.

STORYSELLING™ THE COMMUNITY

Tracy now took the next big step in ensuring the success of his Branded Film - and that was getting the community involved in its production, so they would have a personal stake in its success. Social media updates continued to build the buzz.

That process continued with his social media updates, as well as setting up a story about the film with *The Winston-Salem Journal*. The newspaper even called me for an interview - before I had even come into town to start production. Here's an excerpt from the published piece which appeared in the paper (and online) on June 18th, 2011:

"Frank Myers Auto Maxx is known for its flashy commercials, patriotic Uncle Frank mascot and 'Everybody Rides' slogan. Next week, a film crew will be at the lot on Patterson Avenue, but they won't be filming another quirky commercial. Instead, they will be making a documentary.

We were hushed for almost six months and couldn't say anything about it,' said Tracy Myers, the dealership's owner.

The documentary will be part of a series of films that will focus on businesses and people. It will be produced by Celebrity Films, an entertainment company based in Orlando and Los Angeles.

The film will look at the history of the dealership and Tracy Myer's 'uphill battle' to grow Frank Myers Auto Maxx, said

Nick Nanton, a co-owner of Celebrity Films and a producer and director. Nanton recently received two Emmy nominations for the short film 'Jacob's Turn,' the story of a boy with Down syndrome and his love of baseball."

Besides the newspaper story and press releases, Tracy also invited area people to actually be a part of the film, with social media updates like the following:

Nick came in with the crew (and, of course, Tracy had a news crew waiting for our arrival at his house) and spent about two and a half days filming around Winston-Salem and interviewing Tracy and his family, keeping our StorySelling™ principles in mind as we did so. Our vision combined with the personalities of the Myers family created a lot of memorable moments that would add up to a terrific film. Not only that, but that news crew I mentioned also shot a whole story about the making of the movie, which ended up airing on News 14, a local 24/7 news channel, which showed the report about our movie about every fifteen minutes over the course of a few days. Tracy, of course, posted a link to the news story on Facebook.

Keep in mind, this was like a free commercial for Tracy and his dealership, *airing constantly on a news channel as a news story*, so it had the weight of credibility - and this is in addition to the fact that the movie was featured in a piece on the front page of the local newspaper. That's the beauty of the Branded Film - its value goes far beyond the film itself just because of its existence. Local media are always looking for exciting stories happening in the area - and the production of a local film about a local business is a guaranteed attention-getter. Tracy's existing media relationships definitely helped, but, in any case, the making of *Car Men* would have been a big deal.

THE RED CARPET PREMIERE

As soon as we left town with what we needed, Tracy began working on how he would premiere *Car Men* to the community in a way that would make the biggest possible splash. Here's how he began that process.

Tracy: Well, we absolutely started talking about a red carpet premiere internally before the film was ever shot, of course... and we started talking to the movie theatres in town as soon as you left. We said, "Hey, we might be able to get you the red carpet movie premiere from this Emmy-winning film director that came to town and shot this documentary..." Well it just took two or three sentences to hook them - and that resulted in three different theatres wanting to actually premiere the movie - at no cost to us - in a matter of weeks.

The one we went with, the one that we partnered with, was the theatre that is very aggressive on Twitter. The second we had the press release about the red carpet premiere, they tweeted it out and they social media-ed that thing to death. Not only that, but the person who ran the movie theatre did a little Flip cam video saying, "Hey we got some great news. We just got word that we're premiering the documentary of Winston-Salem business owner Frank Myers Auto Maxx." With the 4000 local followers they had on their Twitter feed, they got the ball rolling really, really quickly.

Tracy Myers
October 22, 2011

Here is part of the poster for the movie "Car Men". World Premier right here in Winston Salem, NC on November 17th at the a/perture Cinema! We are getting excited! — with Ashley Spain and 24 others.

Like · Comment · Share   👍 8 💬 14 🔲 1

You should notice that, once again, just like he did with the local media, Tracy got the movie theatre to not only host his movie premiere for free, but he also inspired them to promote it to the hilt. And Tracy didn't stop there. Once we set the date of the premiere, which was November 17th, 2011, he put out his own press release giving the details of the big night and also saying that people had to quickly request their tickets because seating was going to be limited to first come, first served. Another stroke of genius - because he instantly created scarcity and a higher value to the premiere tickets.

Tracy Myers
October 25, 2011

No one realized the overwhelming response we would have for the world premier of the film "Car Guys". So they've opened up some more seats! All seats, other than the ones for the family & folks involved with the film, are being issued via lottery. To throw your name in the hat, go HERE: http://www.facebook.com/event.php?eid=210089275728513 and leave a message on the official "Car Men" event FB wall. Good luck.

Tracy's premiere night went spectacularly. We provided them with a professional *Car Men* movie poster to put up at the theatre and, on the red carpet, Tracy had video shot of interviewers talking to the guests, as well as crowd reactions of the people watching the movie inside the theatre. The mayor attended as well as many other local community leaders. You can see the results in the video Tracy posted on YouTube at www.TheCarMenMovie.com and, of course, shared all over his multiple social media channels.

Plus, all this publicity made all the people who *didn't* get tickets to the red carpet premiere very excited about seeing the movie. They found themselves left out of this event, which made them really, really want their chance to see it. Which gave the movie even more buzz around town.

There's no question a red carpet premiere of your own Branded Movie can be the kind of once-in-a-lifetime event that will bond your customers to you forever. And it has a certain celebrity cachet that other kinds of promotional events can't quite match. For example, many financial advisors host steak dinners for potential clients so they can sell them their products or services. But how much cooler is it to say, "I'd love you to be my guest at the red carpet premiere of a documentary that was shot on my life and my story. My treat. If you want a ticket, e-mail me. We'll have wine and food there, and I think you'd really enjoy the film, as it will help you understand where I'm coming from, as well as the atmosphere—it's gonna be exciting!"

TAKING IT TO TV AND DVD

Of course, the *Car Men* publicity train wasn't going to shut down after the red carpet premiere. Tracy immediately began publicizing the coming DVD release, which was set to happen two months after the premiere, through more press releases and social media updates, and then hit on another way to garner him and his dealership even more attention with his Branded Film. And again, at virtually no cost to himself.

He approached the local TV stations to see if they would air *Car Men* in advance of the DVD release - not as a paid infomercial, but as local programming - there's very little on those local stations with that level of quality, especially about hometown subject matter. He did that by, again, creating scarcity and adding value to his Branded Film just as he did with his potential red carpet audience - by making the conversation with the stations, "Well, maybe we could let you air this - what would you think about that?"

The local NBC affiliate is the biggest player in the Winston-Salem TV market and they agreed to air it as programming at no cost to Tracy - and they scheduled it for a Sunday at midday. If Tracy had paid for that time, it would have cost him literally thousands of dollars for the half-hour. Tracy, of course, publicized the film's airing heavily, creating a huge amount of social media buzz; and that Sunday, when he came home from church, that buzz blew up.

> **Tracy:** *My e-mail blew up. My Facebook blew up. My Twitter blew up. All locally. On Monday or Tuesday, the television station called and said, "You're not going to believe this." And I said, "I'm not going to believe what?" He said, "Your film beat everybody in the time slot. You were number*

one in the time slot. It even beat the NFL pregame show on CBS." To me, it was unbelievable and unheard of. So we were more than excited.

This started another snowball rolling downhill, because Tracy, of course, publicized his huge ratings in another press release - and, suddenly, two other local affiliates wanted to air the Branded Film. Since the NBC affiliate didn't ask for any kind of exclusive deal, there was no problem with that. Those two stations actually began running the program *repeatedly* - again *absolutely for free* - weekday mornings in the 6 am - 7 am time slots, as well as on Saturdays and Sundays.

Tracy Myers shared Tracy Myers's photo.
January 28

The tv edition of the film "Car Men" is showing TODAY, Saturday, at 12 noon on WXLV in the Triad area of NC. Check it out!

Just Announced! The Winston Salem ABC affiliate, ABC45, and the Winston Salem My TV affiliate, My48, have both agreed to show the television edition of the film "Car Men". The schedule is as follows:
WXLV- Wed January 25 at 6am
WXLV-Thurs January 26 at 6am
WMYV-Friday January 27 at 6:30am
WMYV-Saturday January 28th at 12:00pm
WMYV-Sunday January 29 at 10:30am
WMYV-Monday January 30 at 6:30am
WMYV-Tuesday January 31 at 6:30am

If you haven't seen the movie yet, then this is your chance to do so before the dvd is released!

Now Tracy's dealership was getting thousands upon thousands of dollars worth of free promotion on the local TV stations due to his investment in his Branded Film. And he still had a DVD release coming.

Of course, you might ask, well, how do you get anyone interested in buying a DVD of something that's constantly been on TV? Easy. You just do what all the Hollywood studios do with their DVD releases - create a "Special Edition" of the film with extra never-before seen footage!

Tracy added interviews and footage done on the night of the red carpet premiere to create a longer version of *Car Men* that would only appear on the DVD release - giving even more ongoing value to the product. This additional footage, far from being just padding, actually adds more power to his Branded Film - because those interviews from premiere night featured people saying such things as, "Hey, I've known Tracy for years." "I first met him in the 4th grade." and "I was his Sunday School teacher." They provided more StorySelling™ that further cemented Tracy to his community and his customer base in an authentic and effective way.

Now Tracy was not only selling copies of the DVD to those who wanted to order it for $9.97, but he was also able to use that DVD as a marketing tool to potential customers. Potential leads often called in for more information - and Tracy's people would get their address and send them out the DVD, along with a bag of microwave popcorn. Those people would then watch the Branded Film, which StorySells Tracy and his dealership on a totally different level than any dealership has ever been sold before, and become undoubtedly swayed towards doing business there.

And by the way, the weekend that the DVDs arrived at Tracy's dealership also happened to be Super Bowl weekend. So guess what program the local NBC affiliate aired as their Super Bowl lead-in? If you haven't guessed by now, take a look below...

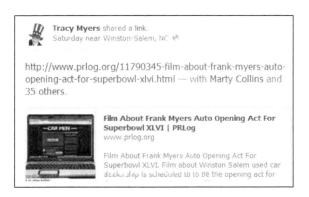

WHY QUALITY COUNTS IN A BRANDED FILM

Everything in this case study worked as well as it could to promote Tracy and his dealership brand. A lot of that is due to Tracy's tireless efforts - but he couldn't have made the impact he did if *Car Men* appeared to be a quickie second-rate production. Tracy made that point very well when he remembered the night of the movie theatre premiere:

When you're there, watching it, it looks like a film when it's on the big screen. It doesn't look like a television show or a cheap production that's been half put-together. It looks like something you would actually see in the movie theatre.

It looks that way because we made sure we had the experience, the talent and expertise to produce his Branded Films as it should be produced. We don't say that to brag, but to emphasize how critical it is to maintain a high standard of quality in these productions. That quality has to extend from properly structuring the StorySelling™ narrative before you begin filming, to the actual filming and post-production on the movie itself.

You can't fake this level of production. You can't hire some guy who shoots news footage at the local station to film some random interviews and hope it all comes together in the editing room; otherwise, you're wasting time and money. It's important to deliver a Branded Film that looks like the real deal - not a phony sales tape that pretends to be about something genuine. *Car Men* is genuine in its content. How genuine?

One more comment from Tracy:

I've heard the feedback from the people that have watched it. Most of those folks would tell me if it were really bad, especially some of the folks, like my dad, who is brutally honest. And he's cried every time he's watched it.

StorySelling™ works only when you tell the right story in the right way. And that's the story behind the success of Tracy Myers and his Branded Film, *Car Men*.

ACT III

STORYSELLING™
IN ACTION
Realizing Results

"A story has its purpose and its path. It must be told correctly for it to be understood."

~ Marcus Sedgwick

CHAPTER 11

CEMENTING YOUR STORYSELLING™
Gaining Internal and External Control

So, in the middle of 1999, the entrepreneur had just cashed out of one Internet start-up and was thinking about what his next venture would be – when a friend left a message asking him if he was interested in investing in an online business that would sell shoes. Even though the dotcom bubble was at its peak, he was inclined to delete the voicemail and move on. It sounded like, as he put it later, "the poster child of bad Internet ideas."

But, when he was confronted with the fact that footwear was a forty-billion-dollar-a-year business at the time, and that mail order sales already accounted for five percent of those sales, he rethought the offer and decided to make the investment after all. They structured the company with a "drop shipment" business model – meaning that they have customer orders fulfilled by different vendors who had their own inventory and the warehouses to store it in. That way the new venture wouldn't need a lot of infrastructure and the risk was relatively low.

The "dotcom bubble" popped big-time the very next year – but the shoe company was still standing. It brought in over a million dollars in sales in 2000 and quadrupled that amount in 2001. The entrepreneur began to see that this could work – and decided to become more involved as Co-CEO. The company opened a small warehouse/fulfillment center and began to service some orders themselves. And he began to develop both a vision and a goal for the company.

The goal? To achieve one billion dollars in annual sales by the year 2010 – and to make *Fortune* magazine's "100 Best Companies to Work For" List. The vision? They would no longer be a company that just sold shoes: they would be a company that provided the best possible customer service – that just *happened* to sell shoes.

To fulfill that vision, they would have to eliminate drop shipping entirely – otherwise, they could not control the complete customer experience. Drop shipping at that time accounted for a quarter of their total income – but, in his mind, the long-term vision was more important than the short-term loss, so he took the hit.

They retrained their customer service agents out of any bad habits they may have picked up at other companies, such as keeping calls as short as possible to make as many sales as possible. Instead, agents were directed to give customers lengthy advice, even to the point of sending them to competitors' websites if they couldn't meet their needs. The company also put new hires through a four week "customer loyalty" training program – and then, after that program was completed, they made those new hires an incredible offer.

The company would pay them two thousand dollars to *quit*.

Why? Well, if the new employee didn't really care about what company they worked at, they would take the money and run. However, if they responded to the company culture, if they felt like this was the place for them, they would stay and be dedicated to the company's vision.

Over 97% turned down the two grand.

And those that stayed were treated very well: The company provided their employees with free lunches, no-charge vending machines, a company library, a nap room, and free health care. The employee satisfaction level rose and so did the customer satisfaction level. The good vibes spread.

By the year 2008, the entrepreneur met one of his goals two years early – the company hit one billion dollars in annual sales. And the next year he met part two of his goal, as the company made the *Fortune* list of the 100 best companies to work for.

Tony Hsieh, the entrepreneur, had built Zappos into an incredible inspiration to the business world with its unique customer service ethos. And in November 2009, Amazon bought the company for close to 1.2 billion dollars total with the understanding that it would still operate independently with its vision left intact.

ORGANIZATIONAL STORYSELLING™

In the first two sections of this book, we analyzed why stories have such a powerful effect on people - and what elements you need to take into account to create your own narrative for your StorySelling™ purposes.

This section takes us to the final stage of StorySelling™ – putting it into action in your day-to-day business activity. This stage begins by determining how to implement your StorySelling™ both *internally*, within your organization, and *externally*, when communicating with your customers.

We began this chapter with the Zappos saga because it is a perfect example of how to accomplish both tasks to the ultimate extent possible. We've helped many of our clients gain access to Tony Hsieh and his StorySelling™ philosophy over the years, because there are few companies that have branded themselves so effectively and with such quick success.

Nick interviewed Tony a couple of years ago, and we will be sharing excerpts of that talk throughout this chapter, beginning with this exchange that perfectly captures the necessity for StorySelling™:

***Nick:** I've heard a quote from you about Zappos being a service company that just happens to sell shoes. Obviously, you're going way beyond that now. I'd love you to talk about that for a second because most people get caught up and think, "If I'm a widget maker, I make widgets, and that's what I do."*

***Tony:** Well, my advice for any business or entrepreneur is whatever you're doing, just think bigger. There is always a bigger vision than whatever it is that you're doing. So take the railroads, for example, they were a great business at one point, and then cars came along, airplanes came along and now they're not such a great business.*

Part of the problem was they thought of themselves as being in the train business, whereas if they thought of themselves as being in the transportation business then they would probably be much better off and would've thought beyond just railroad tracks. Similarly for us, we actually started out just thinking we were in the shoes business, online shoe retail, and then we sat around one day and we thought, okay, the bigger vision would be customer service. If we build the Zappos brand around the very best customer service, then we're not limiting ourselves to just shoes.

What Tony is saying, if we can be excused for translating his words into the terminology of this book, is that *StorySelling™ elevates your business, whatever it may be, into something more than that business.* Zappos' logline became, "We may sell shoes, but we're really about providing the most amazing customer service on the planet." Their narrative became, "We don't care what it costs us in extra employee costs, training, time and even sales, we are going to break the 'normal' business sales mold and do whatever it takes to meet our customers' needs." Or, in the words of Tony:

Tony: We actually take most of the money that we would've spent on paid marketing or paid advertising and put it into the customer experience. So whether it's the things you talked about, like the shipping back and forth, running our warehouse 24/7, or running our call center 24/7 — all of those things are very expensive. But we really think of those as our marketing dollars and let our customers basically do the marketing for us through word of mouth and their loyalty.

Now, let's drill deeper into how they brought that story to life – and how you can do the same with yours.

THE INSIDE JOB

Whether it's just you, you and an assistant, you and a staff, or you and an entire corporation, if you want your StorySelling™ to be as powerful as possible, you must work from "the inside out." If you and anyone else who represents your organization don't believe in your narrative, you may be talking the talk, but you're definitely not walking the walk – and, sooner or later, your customers are going to know it.

For example, Google exemplifies innovation simply because most of us are aware of how they encourage it within the company, giving employees extra time to work on their own projects, even if it has nothing to do with their current job. That's how they developed many of the most popular current Google products, including the driverless car, which is about as far from their core product line as you can get.

In order to create that kind of internal StorySelling™, you have to hire people who fit into the culture you want to create – and properly train them in that culture. Here's more from Tony on that subject:

Nick: I've read a few things about your hiring process… can you tell us about that?

Tony: Yeah, so we actually do two sets of interviews for everyone we hire to work at our headquarters here in Las Vegas. The hiring manager and his/her team interview for the standard experience, technical ability and so on. But then our HR department does a separate set of interviews purely for a cultural fit, and they have to pass both in order to be hired. So we've actually passed on a lot of really smart, talented people that we know can make an immediate impact on our top or bottom line, but if they're not a culture fit we won't hire them.

And the reverse is true as well. We'll fire people if they're bad for the culture, even if they're doing their specific job function perfectly fine. And as far as the training goes, everyone hired goes through the same training that our call center reps go through. It is four weeks long, and we go over company history, our philosophy about customer service and points of company culture. And then they are actually on the phone for two weeks taking calls from customers. After that you start the job that you're actually hired to do.

Here are FOUR big action steps to take in order to ensure you and your employees are creating the story you want to tell within your company:

I. Clearly Articulate Your Core Values

This is the big one. Your core values should become the bedrock of your StorySelling™. We help clients create and implement them in such a way that they become essential components of their narrative.

Of course, we're sure you've seen big corporations paste giant meaningless blocks of copy on their websites and *call* them core values; and we all immediately recognize that some copywriter has been hired to make up some nice-sounding words that sound really good, but actually have little to do with how they do business. That makes it difficult for the StorySeller, because cynicism is the instant reaction to that kind of verbiage.

That's why it's crucial that you create core values that are *understandable, relatable and actionable.*

For example, below you'll find the ten core values that Zappos promotes. You'll see the language is very natural and the messages are very clear:

- Deliver WOW Through Service
- Embrace and Drive Change
- Create Fun and A Little Weirdness
- Be Adventurous, Creative, and Open-Minded
- Pursue Growth and Learning
- Build Open and Honest Relationships With Communication
- Build a Positive Team and Family Spirit
- Do More With Less
- Be Passionate and Determined
- Be Humble

As you can see, that's not a lot of corporate gobbledygook: these are terse, straightforward thoughts written in a conversational language that's easily understood by everyone within the company.

Consider this approach (but do not just copy someone else's core values—it never works—you need to seriously consider what is unique to your company and your vision) when breaking down your narrative into bullet points for those inside your operation to take on board – and for those *outside* your operation to read and admire. In the next chapter, you'll discover how one entrepreneur created his StorySelling™ success from his core value statements.

II. Make the Abstract Actionable

It's one thing to say "Deliver WOW Through Service" – it's another to make it happen. Whatever your core values happen to be, you need to put in place concrete methods to transform those values into real habitual business behavior, both by employees and yourself.

For example, here's how Tony made sure that a customer service representative had a genuine interaction with a customer instead of a programmed one that might be more efficient on a business level, but less satisfying on a human level:

> **Tony:** *Our approach is no scripts and not to measure efficiency in terms of the call times, which is how most call centers are run. Instead, we focus on the culture and make sure everyone in the company understands our long-term vision about building a Zappos brand to be about the very best customer service. We make sure to give them the proper training to use all the tools and so on. But then leave it up to them to just be real and genuine and passionate when they're actually talking to customers. They know the goal when a customer hangs up is for the customer to walk away thinking, "Wow, that was the best customer service I've ever had."*

Incidentally, Disney is another great example of a company that excels at this kind of approach in its theme parks, training its "Cast Members" thoroughly in how to deal with the public in a way that reflects the Disney philosophy.

III. Hold Everyone Accountable to Your Narrative (Most of All, Yourself!)

As we noted, the usual statement of corporate values isn't taken seriously by employees or even management; it's usually more of a public relations ploy rather than any substantial initiative. When it comes to StorySelling™, however, your narrative must be taken seriously by all concerned. There should be incentives for masterfully following through on that narrative – and consequences for violating it.

IV. Keep Your Narrative Alive Internally on an Ongoing Basis

You know the old saw about sharks: They have to keep moving forward or they die. Your StorySelling™ narrative is no different – which is why it's important to find ways to keep it a living, breathing animal through constant attention.

For instance, Zappos publishes a yearly "Culture Book" that runs up to 480 pages long and continues to reinvigorate their StorySelling™. Here's Tony on this ingenious innovation:

__Nick:__ I understand you actually publish a "culture book" about the culture of working at Zappos.

__Tony:__ Yeah, it's a book we put out once a year. We ask all of our employees to write a few paragraphs about what the Zappos culture means to them, and, except for typos, it's unedited. So you get to read both the good and bad. It's organized by department, so you can tell the difference between the different subcultures of different departments. And I guess the way to think about it is — you know how on websites there are customer reviews? These are basically kind of like employee reviews of the company. And we give it to prospective job candidates and even customers, vendors and business partners, just so people can get a pretty good sense of what our culture is like.

The above four action steps create the kind of culture that supports your narrative, rather than subverts it. And that's to your benefit: The secret here is that StorySelling™ doesn't just grow your business on the customer side – it also strengthens it internally. If you implement it effectively, you'll find your employees will feel as if they're part of something bigger than just another business. In turn, they'll be more motivated to fulfill your narrative, they'll work together more efficiently and you'll find yourself with a happier and more productive operation.

TAKING IT TO THE STREETS

If you have your *internal* StorySelling™ tactics in place, then it's time to deliver your narrative to the outside world in a unified and consistent way. Every time you interact with the public is in reality an opportunity to solidify your StorySelling™ and cement your logline with customers and clients.

Apple, of course, is a textbook example of how to make this happen. Through every aspect of its external operation – from their stores to their marketing to their actual products – the elements of coolness and innovation are on full display. Now, in contrast to Zappos, you may hear some complaining about their customer service – but that's not an integral part of their narrative, so they don't have to sweat it as much.

Obviously, you want all aspects of your business to work as well as possible – but you want to make doubly sure that you excel to the full extent of whatever aspect your StorySelling™ emphasizes.

Here are a few *external* areas where it's essential that your narrative takes center stage:

- **Your Marketing and Advertising**

  We're going to delve into this arena in much more detail in Chapter 13, but suffice it to say that you need to make sure none of your marketing efforts contradicts your overall StorySelling™ strategy. An ad agency may have the most brilliant idea for a TV commercial in the world – but if that commercial directly conflicts with the storyline people have already accepted about you, you're in trouble: The public will reject the message and possibly even get angry at you.

  For example, KFC actually tried a campaign in 2003 that advertised how *healthy* their food was. Nobody believed their claims and an *Advertising Age* writer called it "desperate and sleazy." The reason the fast-food chain finally pulled the ad? "Brand protection."[1]

---

1 Kate MacArthur, "KFC Pulls Controversial Health-Claim Chicken Ads," *Advertising Age*, November 18, 2003

• **Your Corporate Communications**

How you interact with the public as a company is also vitally important to your StorySelling™ efforts. For example, if you're positioning yourself as a slightly secretive and mysterious organization in order to hype whatever your next new product or service is, you might want to limit any exposure to the absolute minimum. For example, the Segway, the motorized upright two-wheeled device for pedestrians, is frequently the butt of jokes these days; however, before it was released, its development was very top-secret – and, to facilitate some high-profile leaks that would create a lot of excited anticipation, it was only shown to such luminaries as Steve Jobs (who said it was "as big a deal as the Internet") and billionaire John Doerr (who said it was more important than the Internet!). The pre-release hype and mystery was so huge that the irreverent Comedy Central series *South Park* did a whole episode about it.

In contrast, Zappos, of course, took a completely different approach to its corporate communications, based on its StorySelling™ narrative – by enthusiastically embracing transparency:

Tony: One of our core values is about being as open and honest and as transparent as possible. So we do that with our employees. We share lots of data with our vendors and we have tours that come through every day. They spend a full day or sometimes two days with us and they're listening on calls and see how we score them or spend a few hours with our recruiting team and we share the actual interview questions we ask and so on.

So were very open with everything, and, in fact, we've actually even developed a subscription service out of it for $40 a month at ZapposInsights.com. We share everything by video. You can download the answers to questions that have already been asked or ask any question you have. Then we get the best person at Zappos to answer it. If it's a recruiting *question, we'll get the head of recruiting to answer it, put it on video, transcribe it and then not only are we answering your question but it's made available to everyone else. Over time we're building up a library and a collection of videos that share anything that people want to learn about how we do things.*

- **Content**

Another very effective way to convey your story is to create content that explains and promotes your StorySelling™ narrative; this content can come in the form of books, articles, blogs, videos, speaking engagements and one-on-one interviews. Content like this positions you as more of a thought leader rather than just another business person out for free publicity – and, just as importantly, your vision is seen as the innovative business strategy that it is rather than a marketing gimmick.

We are big believers in this concept – and we work hard to place our clients in such major media outlets as CNN, CNBC, FOX News, the major network affiliates (NBC, CBS, ABC and FOX) and in such national publications as *USA Today, Inc. Magazine, Newsweek, Forbes, The New York Times* and others. These aren't ads we're talking about – this is substantive content that showcases these entrepreneurs and their visions. This exposure is, of course, important to increasing their visibility – but from a bottom-line profit point of view, it's more important as a demonstration to their current and potential customers of their prestige and recognition in the world at large.

The bottom line is that if you can make the media a partner in your StorySelling™, why wouldn't you grab that opportunity? Content is the best way to make that happen. Just ask Tony Hsieh – do you think he would have done that interview with us if he wasn't trying to accomplish just that?

The real takeaway we want you to have from this chapter is you should never look at StorySelling™ as a kind of coat you can just put on and take off when convenient; instead, it has to be seen as an integral part of both your internal and external business image. While some lapses in your StorySelling™ narrative are inevitable, they should be minimal and quickly corrected.

Because your internal/external StorySelling™ structures are really going to be of primary importance moving forward, we're going to spend a little more time on it. We recognize that many of you reading this book aren't doing business on the scale of a Zappos (at least, not yet!) – so next, we'll share a case study of a smaller entrepreneur who built his unique success based on his StorySelling™ core values – and really got his business in shape in more ways than one!

CHAPTER 12

STORYSELLING™ AND CORE VALUES
The Results Fitness Case Study

Alwyn (pronounced Alan…it's just the funny Scottish spelling!) and Rachel Cosgrove are fitness trainers and owners of Results Fitness, a gym located in Santa Clarita, California that's rated as one of the country's ten best by *Men's Health* magazine. We've been working with the Cosgroves for some time and have admired how they've implemented the kind of StorySelling™ principles we're discussing in this book to launch their business up to a whole new level of success.

In this chapter, we'd like to share excerpts from a lengthy recent interview Nick did with Alwyn about how he translated his core values into a StorySelling™ slam-dunk. As we noted in the last chapter, we help clients create and implement their core values for StorySelling™ purposes. This interview gives you a very sharp insight into how Results Fitness created their core values, what they are, how they created a winning culture, and how Alwyn holds his staff (and himself) accountable for maintaining them on a day-to-day basis.

We're going to jump right in with how Alwyn basically figured out creating a unique narrative was what would set his business apart (and, by the way, as Alwyn is Scottish, you'll have to imagine everything he says having a "wee bit of a burr").

Nick: *Let's start with how you figured out the marketing of your business, because we all know that the higher you climb, the more the marketing advantage really allows you to set yourself apart.*

Alwyn: *Absolutely. There are three main parts to any business and I liken them to the three legs of a stool. First, you have marketing, which is your lead generation stuff. People have to know about you. People have confused marketing with advertising; it's way more than that. It's about getting your message out there. It's not just ads. Second, you've got sales, where you can convert these leads to clients, and then, third, you have operations.*

The problem with most businesses is that people tend to focus more on operations and they lose everything else. You've got to focus on all three! The three-legged stool falls over if you take one leg away.

Now, fitness has been around for centuries, but most fitness trainers are what we call "first-generation": They didn't learn under another trainer, so it's a very young field. Very quickly I realized that we had to stop pretending that this was a hobby, and realize this was a business.

So - I started to look at what could I do to make my business different. And it was difficult. You've never seen a personal trainer on a television show in a positive light, right? Whether it's a reality show, a comedy show, or dramatic shows like Law and Order or a CSI, they are always shown in a negative light.

So, my primary question was "How do we change the way fitness is done?" Well, there's a little town in Scotland called Bathgate. Bathgate has a population of

16,000 people, and yet, in a ten-year period, the Bathgate Tai Kwon Do School won 60 Great Britain national titles, 21 European titles, seven world titles, and three additional world medals. Now in that same time frame, the U.S. won about three world medals in these areas.

Of course, it doesn't make any sense that there's more talent in this little town, but it does make sense that there's something happening in the gym located there that's different from any other gym - an intangible.

So I began examining a lot of businesses asking the question, "Who's the best in each field? Who is the number one in each category?" I came up with Nike, Virgin, Ritz-Carlton, Apple, Starbucks, Disney, Nordstrom…innovative companies like that. I then asked myself, "What makes these guys number one, and how can I apply it to the gym business?"

The answer that came back when I dug deeply: All these have a different culture. That Tae Kwon Do School in Scotland is not teaching different fighting techniques. They just have a culture where it's the toughest gym in the world. That's where people would gravitate to and the training would continue to improve. There are probably boxing gyms in Detroit, and the Kronk Gym, which have had the same idea – this idea of a strong culture.

I started realizing that the reason these guys were successful is that they understood branding, but that branding was based on core values – they are really an operating system for how you do it. When I started understanding that, I started to connect the dots with what I needed to understand: marketing is about your story.

So - what is my story? My story is about the culture in our gym and the core values that we have. Regardless of what your business is, I think it's important to understand that marketing is about getting your story out there.

Nick: *Amen. And when it comes to core values, they should be internal, but they also need to be externalized for customers to see as well. This allows the consumer and the employees to be on the same page, which is a huge need in today's marketplace. Most of the time, the communications inside and the communications outside don't really match, but, by putting together a good set of core values and telling a story, you allow everything to come into alignment. Also, if you have a strong set of core values, it becomes so much easier to make decisions because you just have to ask, "Does this fit with our core values or not?"*

Alwyn: *That's how we make our decisions. I mean lots of companies have core values written on the walls when you go in. But they may as well be written down the toilet, because no one follows them. You've got to make a commitment to it. I think that our story for Results Fitness is that we saw there was a problem in the fitness industry and we decided to change the way fitness is done; and here's what we stand for, this is our story, do you want to be part of it?*

Nick: *And that's genius in and of itself. Everybody wants to belong to something bigger than themselves – and you're inviting a prospect into a whole new world. I don't think anyone has created the mindset of "Do you want to join us in changing the fitness world?"*

Alwyn: *Yup, and that's how we do it. And not everybody can be part of the family, and that's all right. But here's what we stand for, here's where we're going and this is what we want to do.*

I read something that Richard Branson said a long time ago and that was that he will only do stuff if he can do it better - and be an innovator. He's not going to do something the same as everybody else just to get in the game. We're in the business of solving problems. Our product is fitness, but someone comes with a problem and we deliver that solution through a culture that demands success and supports success - everything elevates when you do that. Whether you are running a real estate firm or a car dealership, what do you believe in? What are you trying to do? If you are just about making money, there are easier ways.

*I think on some level this comes from the book **Peak** by Chip Conley, where he talks about Maslow's <u>Hierarchy of Needs</u>. He says employees need to make money just to get by, but, after they reach a certain level, they are no longer motivated by money, they are motivated by recognition. But the top level, at the peak of the pyramid, is this desire to commit and belong to something bigger than themselves. That's the idea that we put into everything we do. For example, in our Results Fitness number one best-selling book, people were expecting for me to talk about exercising - but I discussed culture instead. I mean that's the missing link. If you're having a five figure income, you can't just do more of what you are doing and get a six figure income. If you've got a six figure income, you can't just do more and get a seven figure income. You have to do something different - and the missing link just might be this internal operating system of core values and culture.*

Nick: *There are eleven of your core values that I've seen on your website. I can read them; I think they're important to hear....*

Alwyn: *I've memorized them. They're internal.*

Nick: *Wow. It's certainly a daunting task to create them in the first place. I think everyone thinks, "Man I'm just going* *to take that person's core values, those are great." But that usually doesn't work out…*

Alwyn: *Actually, there's a gym somewhere in the country that took our core values and, word for word, put them on their site. Now, this does not upset me, I think that's amazing that I can influence people like that, but it's not real. That person didn't think these through and say, "Do I truly believe in these?"*

Anyway, here are our core values. Number one is: "Bring your best." Our staff has got to do their best every day. That's all I ask. If you come in tired and sleepy, you're not bringing your best…and time is the only limited resource that we have in this life. That's the only thing that we cannot increase. You can get more money, you cannot get more time. So if you come one day, to one shift, without bringing your best, that day is gone forever. So number one is always bring your best.

Nick: *Real quick, just one thing that I want to talk about is that the positioning of accountability changes completely from employer to employee when you have core values like that one. Instead of going and berating someone, or even just trying to figure out how to explain to them that they didn't do well enough, it's such an easy thing to say, "Hey, what's your number one core value? Bring your best. You tell me, did you bring your best on that?" It's just interesting that you can play on the same team but teach the lesson at the same time.*

Alwyn: *Yeah. That's the thing. Moving on, number two is:* "Be professional." *Number three is:* "Be honest and transparent," *and Number four is: "Communicate clearly with mutual understanding." That last one wasn't there originally. We had to add that because we were noticing that we were dropping the ball on that a little bit. So these* *values are dynamic – and they're all action statements.*

Number five I stole from Lance Armstrong: "Have only good days and great days." The gym needs to be the high point of our members' day. Doing business with us, no matter what business you are in, should be the best part of your customers' day - even if you're selling cheeseburgers at the diner. You should be the high point of their day if you're doing it right. I know you're saying that you can't be the high point in everybody's day, but that's my goal.

Nick: *Cool.*

Alwyn: *Number six is, "Be 'we' not 'me'" – that's the teamwork part of it. We work as a team, there are no stars. They're not my staff, they're my team and I'm just part of the team. Just as a quick aside, we did a seminar a couple of years ago, which was like a transformation contest, and one of the previous winners stood up and gave a little talk about how well she'd done. One of my team members put up his hand and said, "Hey, who was your trainer during this time?" She responded, "Well, it was you" and kind of made a joke about it. I was not happy - because it's not him. He didn't get the client, he didn't sign up the client, he didn't put the program in place, he didn't bill the client and handle the scheduling; he executed the training system. He was just part of the wheel and he needed to recognize that. So that's something that we take very seriously.*

Number seven is: "Constantly learn, always improve." We've got to stay sharp; you've got to keep working on your game. Number eight is: "Have fun and a sense of humor." If you've been around me for any length of time you know that there's no way I'm going through the day without cracking up at least once. Number nine is: "Be profitable."

Nick: *That is on the wall for customers to see as well, right?*

Alwyn: *Absolutely.*

Nick: *I love that, but some people might not, they might think that's kind of a negative thing to put out in front of your customers. I don't, but let's get into talking about profitability in front of customers.*

Alwyn: *Well, first of all, I want to be honest and transparent and my basic line is that if we do great work, we deserve to be compensated for this great work.*

Nick: *Yes.*

Alwyn: *Now what I didn't say is that we make a profit, I keep it all and spend it all, just me. Because that's not the case. We reinvest in the gym and reinvest in our organization and we raise the standards. But, without profit, everything stops. If I say, "Be honest and transparent" is one of my core values, and then turn around and say, "Be profitable" only behind the scenes, I'm already violating one core value right there.*

Nick: *Okay, cool, I love it, move on.*

Alwyn: *All right, number ten is: "Exceed expectations." This is just the idea that the client has their basic needs that they want met, but we want to go above and beyond all those needs all the time. How can we do this better or faster than anybody else?*

Our last one, number eleven is: "Keep leading." It ties in with Richard Branson's idea that we have to be ahead of the market. We don't have to do everything, but we have to be leading from our industry. We have to continually innovate and do things better and just be the model for the rest of the world to follow as far as fitness goes.

Nick: *I love those and they are so true. Let's talk for a second about where you think that people should begin with creating their own core values for their storytelling, because these are such high level ideas. Where would you suggest somebody start? Where did you start?*

Alwyn: *You have to realize that they are not rules. They're who you already are. You already have core values and you just haven't sort of verbalized them. I started by thinking "What do I believe in, what's important to me?" I remember some friends of mine were going to watch a soccer game on TV at this sports bar near my house and I was flying back from Scotland that afternoon, but I said, "Yeah, I'll come down." They said, "You won't come down, you're going to be tired, you'll be exhausted, you won't be there." I landed and I was tired and I was exhausted - but I went because it's important to me that I do what I say I'll do. I knew that no one would be mad if I didn't go, but I would be mad at myself.*

So it starts with what do you believe in, what's important to you and who do you respect and why. If you start thinking about people who you respect, maybe Richard Branson, Donald Trump, Sugar Ray Leonard, anybody like that, even the pastor at your church, ask yourself, "Why? Why do I respect them?" It's usually because they represent a core value. There is something about them that you respect.

And also get input from your team and what you think the organization is all about. What's your higher purpose? <u>The real part is that it's a commitment to your people.</u> If your business has eleven core values and you have an elite staff member who only takes ten onboard, they have to be let go. You have to live and die by these because if you don't, it's going to come back and bite you.

Your entire team must have every core value on the list to really create your culture. The same goes for clients. If a client or a customer is not for you, if they are ruining the culture or draining the energy, they need to be let go as well. If your customer is negative or is not a part of your culture and your energy and your place, this will come back and haunt you, because they will infect other people and they will ruin what you've built so hard to protect. Most people don't put poison in their body because it will kill them eventually. Don't put poison in your business because it will kill you eventually.

The last part is that you've got to start talking in this language. It's about constant feedback and a relentless reinforcement of how we're talking in core values. I'm not going to reprimand a staff member or write them up based on an incident. It's got to be based on one of the eleven core values.

But you also have to build an environment to support those values. If it's impossible for everyone to work as a team, that's on me, that's not on them, right? So they can write me up. When we do our performance evaluations, we just grade on core values – and they grade me on core values too.

Nick: *Interesting, and how often do you do that?*

Alwyn: *We do that every quarter, every three months. Now, if I take care of our culture and I take care of those rules, everything else falls into place. Retention is good, signing up people is good. Our marketing is all about our message, and our message is about who we are. I could do graphs about scientific training and physiology and overload, but that doesn't tell you anything about what it's like training with us.*

Nick: *And no one gives a damn because they are really there to be treated well, to have a great time, and to get results, right?*

Alwyn: *Yes, and again this culture is the missing link. Everyone with a business is just helping people who have a problem. It's not about our product, it's about us being the solution.*

Nick: *Right. Whether it's a weight problem, a fitness problem, or, say, a transportation problem if you're a car dealer, it's about fixing problems.*

Alwyn: *It's just people have a problem and we are the solution and that's it. There are a lot of businesses out there that are solutions in search of problems, unfortunately. They come up with great ideas that nobody actually wants.*

Nick: *That happens all too often.*

What's impressive about Alwyn's approach is his thoughtfulness in creating his core values and his absolute commitment to making those core values come alive for his clients and his staff. His narrative of doing fitness in a completely different way has paid off for him – because it's more than a narrative, it's how he actually runs his business both internally and externally. Do the same and you can share in his level of success.

And once you do have your StorySelling™ ready to go, it's time to get into the nuts and bolts of your marketing campaigns. We'll look at how you can maximize those marketing results in the next chapter!

CHAPTER 13

MARKETING THROUGH STORYSELLING™
Creating Cumulative Impact

Chemist Dr. Bill Mitchell thought he had created a winner back in 1957 – a sugary, powdered, orange drink that was vitamin-enhanced; kids would love to drink it and parents would love to buy it for them, since it had marketable health benefits. His employer, General Foods, agreed with him.

In 1959, the product finally hit the store shelves – but, despite it being advertised as having more Vitamin C than orange juice, it did not find itself making its way to many American break-fast tables. Families just weren't ready to drink a powder-based beverage in place of real juice. Nor was the new drink able to compete with Kool-Aid or any of the sweet sodas that ruled the snack time beverage market – instead, it seemed to fall through the cracks in the marketplace.

General Foods had a problem on its hands.

Fortunately for the corporation, NASA, the U.S. space agency, had a problem too. The astronauts on its fledging flights com-plained about the bitter taste of the water supply, which was a byproduct of the space capsule's environmental system. When the agency didn't come up with a solution, one astronaut simply brought a packet of Bill Mitchell's creation along for the ride and poured it into the vehicle's water. Flavor problem solved.

And so it was that millions of people watched astronaut John Glenn eat applesauce and drink *Tang*, the name of Bill Mitchell's brainchild, as he became the first man in the world to orbit the earth in February of 1962.

General Foods knew a marketing opportunity when they saw it. And soon, space footage was making its way into Tang commercials, which heavily emphasized the fact, over and over, that this was the beverage *NASA had specifically chosen* for its astronauts to drink on their missions – giving it the appearance of having the approval of the scientific community, even though John Glenn's choice was just a fluke.

Sales blasted off. And, thanks to some clever marketing, so did the perception that Tang, was in fact, *created by* NASA for the space program, giving it even more scientific credibility; it quickly acquired the aura of a cool, futuristic "beverage of tomorrow." A few years later, even after NASA dumped Tang in favor of its own flavorful nutritious concoction, General Foods continued to market it as a cornerstone of the space program. Today, Tang brings in a billion dollars a year in revenue – only the twelfth brand in Kraft Foods' history (the company bought General Foods in 1990) to do so.

And that billion-dollar brand only came to life because of some brilliant StorySelling™.

PROPELLING YOUR STORYSELLING™ MARKETING INTO OUTER SPACE

It's clear from Tang's exemplary example how StorySelling™ can make marketing infinitely more powerful, memorable and impactful. In the sixties, the space race was the coolest undertaking America was involved in; baby boomers like Tom Hanks, who went on to star in *Apollo 13* and produce the HBO mini-series, *From the Earth to the Moon*, grew up obsessed with it. By attaching itself to NASA's efforts, Tang became as cutting-edge and amazing as a man walking on the moon.

Of course, the problem with this particular StorySelling™ direction was that, as the space program began to wind down, so did Tang's popularity (luckily, declining sales in the U.S. have been offset by skyrocketing sales in Asian markets).

That's why, to build lasting value with no expiration date, the StorySelling™ marketing of a Celebrity Brand should be more evergreen in nature; the kind of core values we discussed in the last two chapters play better over the long run. They can also be utilized to play off of current trends and fashions if need be, rather than *just* being about those trends and fashions.

In this chapter, we're going to look at how to StorySell your values creatively and consistently through all aspects of your marketing. And we're going to do that by using as an example a guy who's as good as anybody at doing just that – even though he certainly lacks the futuristic luster of the Tang/NASA combo.

We're talking about Dan Kennedy, the legendary direct marketer, who has built a thriving multi-million dollar business empire through the StorySelling™ process we just described above. In 2012, we were excited to collaborate with Dan on a best-selling book entitled, *Marketing Miracles* – and we can all learn a lot from his example.

With that in mind, let's take a look at some "DO's" and "DONT's" that we've seen Dan apply to his own StorySelling™ marketing over the years – and that you can apply to yours.

#1: *DO* APPLY YOUR CORE VALUES TO YOUR MARKETING

Dan has successfully positioned himself as something of a "throwback," a traditional marketer who shows disdain for today's slick advertising – and who, instead, gives his devotees the "No B.S." truth on marketing. He has taken his old-school approach so far as to state that he doesn't even use email or the internet – he does all his electronic communication by fax! Dan's "herd," as he calls them, loves his eccentricities – as a matter of fact, they help bond his followers closer to his brand, as they feel they "know" Dan on a special level that outsiders don't.

If your StorySelling™ narrative is powerful enough, you should be able to follow Dan's example and use your values and personality consistently in your marketing to attract more and more into your own "herd." You'll build more of a *personal* relationship that takes you beyond simple business-customer transactions to something more lasting and powerful.

#2: *DON'T* SPEAK THE WRONG LANGUAGE

Dan Kennedy uses plain language to communicate in his marketing, because he knows he's mostly talking to conservative guys who are looking for a shortcut to success (although he definitely has a lot of women practicing what he preaches as well). You, in turn, should make sure you're talking in the right way to your audience.

Are your clients more educated and sophisticated? Or do they need to be led by the hand with a simpler approach? Do you need to sound young and innovative? Or older and experienced? Language is critical in your marketing to connect with the right potential leads – so make sure you strike the right tone.

#3: *DO* PLAY THE "NAME GAME"

Think about finding a catchy way to nail your narrative by giving yourself a new nickname you can place prominently in your marketing? For example, Dan calls himself "The Millionaire Maker." We all see countless examples of this every day – for instance, an IRS attorney who might call himself "The Tax Expert" or a dentist who bills herself as the "Smile Specialist."

These nicknames are, many times, easier for people to remember than your real name – just make sure you can lock up the Internet domain name before you settle on one!

#4: *DON'T* OVER (OR UNDER) SELL

Dan's audience *expects* to be sold – they don't mind his continual marketing because that's what he's all about (and, more importantly, they also want to learn from and emulate what he's doing).

Your specific sales approach can range from merely providing potential customers with legitimate and useful content all the way to an over-the-top "Crazy Eddie" style of screaming sales pitch. You have to determine what works best for your specific StorySelling™ narrative – and what your typical client or customer is expecting from you.

#5: *DO* MAKE SURE YOUR STORYSELLING™ HAS THE RIGHT "LOOK"

The visual element of marketing often takes center stage as well in your marketing initiatives. Think of Nike's spare use of its "Swoosh" logo – or Apple's consistently elegant advertising design; in both cases, the brands' visual StorySelling™ registers almost immediately with the viewer, allowing them to get right to the 'meat' of their current message, and meaning they never have to waste time explaining who they are.

Similarly, Dan Kennedy is famous for his "low-tech" approach to his marketing visuals – encasing an information kit in brown paper bagging would not only be accepted but applauded by Kennedy-ites. They don't expect elegance – as a matter of fact, that's something to be distrusted in Kennedy StorySelling™. "No B.S." means no frills when it comes to design (although even Dan has updated his look in recent months, presumably to continue to attract younger followers).

#6: *DON'T* IGNORE ANY OPPORTUNITY TO MARKET YOUR NARRATIVE

Dan Kennedy's attitude pervades everything he does: Whether it's a simple email or a complete book, his narrative is always firmly in place – and is always selling his Celebrity Brand on some level. In previous chapters, we've talked about how other StorySelling™ superstars like Donald Trump and Richard Branson accomplish the same thing with every move they make.

Your StorySelling™ narrative should be suggesting an overall *attitude* that comes through in every marketing move you make, from your LinkedIn profile page to your YouTube videos to your website copy. Check out Dan Kennedy's stuff – and you'll see a clear and consistent tone throughout…which brings us to our final "Don't"…

#7: DON'T VIOLATE YOUR NARRATIVE!

Actor Bill Murray is now known for doing a variety of dramatic movie roles – some of which have gotten him Oscar nominations. However, in 1984, he was mostly known as the goofball lead of such hugely popular lowbrow comedies as *Ghostbusters* and *Stripes*. So, when the actor played the lead in a serious version of W. Somerset Maugham's philosophical novel, *The Razor's Edge*, audiences (and, mind you, they weren't *large* audiences) were confused – and Murray's attempt to alter his StorySelling™ narrative backfired badly at the time.

Similarly, if Dan Kennedy came out with an academic dissertation on marketing, announced he had received his Ph.D. and requested that everyone call him "Dr. Kennedy," many of his followers would be completely thrown for a loop – unless it was some kind of elaborate joke.

Once your audience is accustomed to seeing you a certain way, they are inclined to reject any radical attempt to present you in a different way. As we discussed in Chapter 3, when people buy into a story, their brains will actively fight any effort that *con-*

tradicts that story. That's why you have to be careful in terms of being consistent in your marketing approach.

By the way, this isn't to say you can't change your narrative as you evolve – it's actually smart if you do, as we discussed in Chapter 8. But you have to take baby steps. Murray eventually changed his StorySelling™ image by taking *supporting* dramatic roles that had elements of comedy in them. These were movies that weren't necessarily aimed at Murray's fans - and brought him a whole new audience that would accept him not playing the fool.

The above DO's and DON'T's give you a rough guideline for how to successfully implement your StorySelling™ into your marketing materials. But there's one last all-important step to take in order to make your StorySelling™ really stick....

THE POWER OF REPETITION
IT'S A WONDERFUL DEVICE

Wc all know what happens when a snowball rolls downhill; it continues gathering more and more snow until it grows and grows in mass and force.

That's exactly what happens to your Celebrity Brand when you apply StorySelling™ to all aspects of your marketing. When we say all aspects, we mean *all* aspects - we're talking about:

- **Business cards**
- **Websites**
- **Newsletters**
- **Billboards**
- **Direct mail campaigns**
- **Letterhead**
- **Email signatures**
- **TV ads**

- **Radio ads**
- **Brochures**
- **Promotional items**
- **Social Media**
- **Internet marketing**
- **Online videos**
- **Magazine Ads**
- **Holiday Cards**
- **Logos and Design Elements**

...and whatever other marketing efforts you're planning or already have in place. The idea is to plant the seed of your narrative – even if it's just a slogan – wherever you can.

Let's return to the story with which we began this chapter: This was how, when consumers thought of Tang in the sixties and seventies, they connected it with the story of astronauts drinking it on NASA missions. That association only happened because General Foods hammered home this message again and again, through the type of ads we showed you in the beginning of this chapter, until that narrative was firmly implanted in American minds.

That couldn't have happened with one single advertisement – it had to be done through *relentless repetition.* An old marketing axiom has it that, at the point when you're finally completely sick and tired of your own message, that's just about the time that the public is just *beginning* to pay attention to it. You deal with your marketing constantly, so it's very easy for you to overdose on your own message. However, your public is a different story, and your message is only one of thousands they going to be exposed to on an everyday basis.

That's why you need to create a *cumulative impact* through repetition to really stand out with your StorySelling™ marketing.

If you don't think repetition has power, consider the case of the

Christmas movie classic, *It's a Wonderful Life*. As of this writing, this almost seventy-year-old black and white film is shown yearly on NBC around the holidays; no other film like it gets that kind of first class treatment. Not only that, but many popular TV series continue to reference and spoof its well-known plot – so most of us are probably of the opinion that this movie has *always* been well-known and beloved.

However, in 1974, It's a Wonderful Life was a not-so-wonderful flop that was virtually forgotten; even the owners of the rights to the film didn't think it was worth anything. They failed to renew its copyright that year and the movie entered the public domain.

That meant any TV station in the country could show the movie *without having to pay for it.*

And they did – relentlessly every Christmas. Every first, second and third-rate TV channel would repeat the movie endlessly, simply because they could sell advertising for a couple of hours that cost them nothing to program. Only *then* did *It's A Wonderful Life* – and it's unique narrative – finally become a part of our holiday rituals, so much so that a production company found a way to reclaim the copyright, resulting in NBC paying big bucks to an exclusive long-term deal to license the movie for annual showings.

So – what do you want your StorySelling™ narrative to be? *It's a Wonderful Life* in 1974 or in 2013? The only difference between the two is the element of repetition.

One last note about *It's a Wonderful Life*. As you probably know, it's all about how we can all change the world for the better by making a positive impact. Well, you can do that with StorySelling™ as well.

And we'll reveal how that can happen in the very next chapter.

CHAPTER 14

STORYSELLING™ FOR A CAUSE
Boosting Awareness, Raising Money and Creating Change

All of their parents were worried. And with good reason.

Three kids, only one of whom was old enough to have graduated from college, had bought a used video camera on eBay and decided to go make a film. And even though they all lived in Southern California, this wasn't anything close to a Hollywood project. No, this trio had decided to go to a war-torn area of Africa just to see what they might find.

They didn't have a plan. They certainly didn't have much money. And they had never done anything like it. But they thought they'd make a kind of road movie to document their travels for fun.

The fun soon ended. They ended up stranded in northern Uganda and made what was easily the most horrible discovery of their young lives: Out in the countryside, on a nightly basis, local children were being kidnapped from their families and forced to serve as child soldiers in a mercenary army. Thousands of other local kids, anxious to escape that deadly fate, made a journey of many miles on foot, without shoes, to find shelter in the nearest cities where they had some degree of protection.

The three American boys discovered these desperate youths sleeping practically on top of each other on the floor at a hospital in the Ugandan city they were staying in – and documented the massive group of children in their video. The would-be filmmakers also encountered their own physical risks – all three contracted malaria, causing one of them to lose sixty pounds.

But they finished their almost-no-budget film and premiered it a year later at a San Diego community center – to an audience of five hundred. The response made them want to do more to help; they wanted to increase awareness of what was happening to these kids and try to stop it. They worked to get their movie screened at high schools, colleges and churches. And, in classic Hollywood style, they made a series of sequels.

And finally they started a nonprofit organization, something none of them had ever imagined doing, to help rebuild war-torn schools in Uganda and also provide scholarships to children there.

Other young people joined their movement – one of them convinced his parents to loan the fledging organization $70,000. Out of donated office space in a San Diego industrial park, they began to raise money from their grassroots efforts, which were beginning to snowball. From that $70,000 investment, they were able to create an infrastructure that allowed them to raise millions and millions.

On March 5, 2012, exactly nine years after the threesome made their first journey to Uganda, their organization put up on the Internet their latest production - a professionally-produced half-hour documentary version of the story about the enslaved army of children entitled *Kony 2012*. It instantly went viral everywhere on the web at a pace never before seen, racking up over twenty million views in a matter of weeks and raising both awareness and money for this cause. As of September of 2012, the film had over 93 million views on YouTube and almost 17 million views on Vimeo.

But maybe the most shocking statistic was this: a poll taken shortly after the video's initial release suggested that over *half* of *all* young American adults had heard about the *Kony 2012* film – in a matter of days.

THE NEXT STEP IN STORYSELLING™

Kony 2012, the film created by the nonprofit organization Invisible Children is an incredible demonstration of how StorySelling™ can promote not only a product or a brand, but also a *cause* (and also of how a branded film can have an incredible impact, as we discussed in Chapter 9). *Kony 2012* creates such a compelling narrative that Kony, the Ugandan war criminal who was behind the kidnapping of children for military purposes, isn't even mentioned until nearly a third of the way through the running time – instead, you're drawn in by the children's story and made to feel part of something bigger than yourself.

And that's a process that not only works for nonprofits such as Invisible Children, but also for big brands. For example, Pepsi has a "Refresh" initiative that gave out twenty million dollars in grants for people to promote new ideas that had a positive impact on the world; Starbucks has their Shared Planet program to help communities with environmental programs; and Nike has their Better World subdivision to encourage recycling of its products. There are many more examples of these kinds of corporate causes – but the point is they are putting millions of dollars behind these kinds of projects not just to help the world, but because it's also *good branding*.

In today's marketplace, consumers want to reward the "good guys" more than ever. And that's why, more and more, you see huge companies engaging in cause marketing on a massive scale and promoting them heavily through social media. So consider taking on the right cause yourself – and make it an integral part of your StorySelling™.

This chapter will teach you some very effective ways to do just that, whether you're a nonprofit dedicated to change – or a personal brand wanting to expand your influence.

THE STORYSELLING™ DIFFERENCE

In today's crowded marketplace, the last thing any cause marketer should assume is that, just because they're talking about a worthy subject, everyone's going to automatically pay attention to them.

The fact is, great StorySelling™ is *required* to sell a cause. Would anyone have cared about horrible conditions in Uganda – if the Invisible Children organization hadn't worked so hard to create a *story* that would grab people's attention? There are other human tragedies just as devastating happening around the globe – the difference was that *Kony 2012* expertly conveyed the one in Uganda with some compelling StorySelling™.

That's why we produced *Jacob's Turn* and are continuing to work on other similar projects through our Entrepreneurs International Foundation, such as the branded film we recently created to benefit Esperanza International, an organization that dedicates itself to helping children and their families in the Dominican Republic escape poverty (Esperanza was founded by former Seattle Mariners catcher Dave Valle and his wife Vicky). More broadly, we have also created a system called FilmFunding™ which helps other nonprofits raise the money to produce films to promote their causes.

But again, as we noted, cause marketing is as important to for-profits as it is to non-profits - and StorySelling™ brings three powerful advantages in the ways it can raise awareness (as well as much-needed funds), for a cause marketer:

ADVANTAGE #1:
STORYSELLING™ CREATES EMPATHY

As we've discussed in previous chapters, a well-told story causes the listener to empathize with the "hero" – and to feel what that hero feels in his or her struggle to overcome obstacles. When a documentary tackles a cause, the organization fighting for that cause becomes this "hero." We see the odds it must face in trying to do the good deeds it has set out to accomplish – and we end up rooting for it succeed, just like we'd root for Rocky to win a fight or Iron Man to take out a super-villain threatening the world.

Similarly, when you tell the story of someone who represents the cause in a powerful way, you create a strong emotional bond with that cause. There have been numerous very effective anti-smoking ads over the years featuring long-time smokers who are dying from their tobacco habit. Academy Award-winning actor Yul Brynner even recorded a commercial specifically produced to run on television *after* he passed away from cancer, in which he warned viewers, "Now that I'm gone, I tell you: Don't smoke, whatever you do, just don't smoke."

How many times more powerful is that than a spot made up of statistics and charts about the health risks of smoking? Hard to calculate, but easy to imagine.

ADVANTAGE #2:
STORYSELLING™ PUTS A FACE ON
AN ABSTRACT CAUSE

There is a reason that both the Humane Society's effort to help abandoned animals and charities that solicit sponsorships for im-poverished children in other countries relentlessly run commercials with long close-ups of those they seek to help with some kind of well-known emotional song ("You Are So Beautiful" by Joe Cocker and "I Will Remember You" by Sarah McLachlan) playing throughout the commercial. They're effective – it's hard to turn away from needy kids (or sad dogs!) without feeling you have to do something to help them. This is StorySelling™ at its most basic – putting a *face* (or in this case, many faces) on a cause that you can identify with emotionally.

If you want a pre-online example of how powerful a face can be to a cause, look no further than the AIDS epidemic in the 1980's. The virus had claimed many lives and seemed to be out of control, but then-President Ronald Reagan still made no mention of it. However, when his Hollywood friend, actor Rock Hudson, passed away from the disease in 1985, the President finally addressed the topic and said it was a priority for his administration. At the time, actress Morgan Fairchild said, "Rock Hudson's death gave AIDS a face."[1]

ADVANTAGE #3:
STORYSELLING™ INSPIRES ACTION

For a cause, this is probably the most important advantage StorySelling™ brings to the table. We began this chapter by discussing the Kony 2012 video. When it went viral, so did the cause – to millions of people who didn't even know who Kony was. And Invisible Children's donations *tripled* for the fiscal year ending in June of 2012.

Even Oprah gave the charity two million dollars!

PUTTING STORYSELLING™ TO
WORK FOR YOUR CAUSE

These are pretty heavy-duty advantages to contribute to any cause; that's why so many marketing experts recommend that nonprofits use storytelling in order to make the most impact. If you're wondering how to make StorySelling™ work for your cause, here are a few of the most effective ways:

• **Show Those Who Need Help**
   As we just noted, causes try to raise money in many in-

---

1 "The Show Goes On in Aids Battle," BBC News, November 24th, 2003

stances by simply showing the *faces* of the needy. You can take this method one step further by actually telling the *story* of one person (or animal, for that matter) who's in a life-and-death situation where assistance is desperately needed. Obviously, this is a very effective approach and one that really paid off for the producers of *Kony 2012*.

You can also take more of a focused approach by telling the narrative of one needy person through that individual's point of view. This can actually be more powerful in creating that all-important empathy that sparks action. This method was used repeatedly by Jerry Lewis and the Muscular Dystrophy Association during their yearly Labor Day telethons, when they would show various vignettes of children and how the disease affected their individual lives (and continue to raise record-breaking donation amounts on an annual basis).

• Show Those You've Helped

Organizations such as March of Dimes and Big Brothers Big Sisters have launched social media StorySelling™ efforts that spotlight those whose lives they've helped change for the better. Similarly, the Make-A-Wish foundation shares its video wishes on YouTube.

By showing how your cause initiative actually made a difference, you demonstrate the actual good that donations can do for potential donors. When the public can see their dollars actually impacting lives in dramatically positive ways, they feel much more confident about giving to your cause.

• Use Some Star Power

When Hollywood makes a movie about an actual event or living notable, they don't go out and hire the actual people who were involved to reenact the story; they hire star actors and actresses. Why? Because people *want* to see celebrities.

That's why so many causes try to obtain the services of a

celebrity spokesperson to tell their story – and many celebs are willing simply because it's good for *their* Celebrity Brands. The public is predisposed to pay more attention when a public personality is delivering the message. This, of course, doesn't have to be a TV or movie celebrity – it could be a sports star, a well-liked political figure or other public personality.

Of course, you should choose wisely when using this StorySelling™ method. Bicycling champion Lance Armstrong had to publicly resign from Livestrong, the charity he himself had founded fifteen years ago, to stop the damage caused by accusations that he doped his way to victory to achieve his record-setting race wins.

• What's the Worst that Could Happen?

In the last chapter, we discussed the movie *It's a Wonderful Life* – well, the plot of that film applies to this StorySelling™ method. Think of telling a story where the viewer has to imagine what it would be like if your cause initiative wasn't there to do whatever it does. For example, there have been scores of PSAs that dramatized the stories of those who abuse alcohol and drugs and end up in tragic situations, because no one ever intervened and stopped them.

• Leave Them Laughing

Humor is definitely not always the best way to motivate action, but it can still be effective (you can check out seven funny "message" ads at: http://armchairadvocates. com/2012/07/02/top-7-hilarious-psa-videos-that-mix-humor-and-social-good/). Of course, funny online videos always get a lot of attention, but, again, results from those funny videos can be mixed (which is a reason why a lot of companies actually shy away from humorous advertising).

These are just a few of the most prominent cause marketing StorySelling™ approaches – there are literally millions of them out there, and available to look at on the internet. It's simply a matter of choosing which StorySelling™ narrative will work best for your particular cause and your specific fundraising needs.

Social Media: Your Most Powerful StorySelling™ Venue

Kony 2012 is the star example of StorySelling™ a cause through social media. Most people who discovered the film found it "shared" by Facebook friends or clicked on a Twitter link.

The truth is that, even though cause marketing has been around for a long time, social media has caused it to, in the words of Arianna Huffington, "catch fire."[2] Here are a few eye-opening statistics gathered from MDG Advertising from various sources:[3]

• 98% of nonprofits use Facebook and 74% are on Twitter.

• There was a 91% increase in the amount of donations made on social media from 2011 to 2012.

• 68% of social media users will want to find out more about a cause if a friend posts about it.

• The average value of a "Like" on Facebook, in terms of donations, is an average $161 per. When combined with marketing over other social media sites, that increases to $214.

Why are cause marketing and social media such an amazing match? Because people like to feel part of something positive and life-affirming – and, if they "share" something like the *Kony 2012* film, they feel like they're doing something to combat the problem and they feel good about themselves. "Authenticity" is a key word when it comes to social media – and most causes, of course, are incredibly authentic in their desire to simply make a positive difference in the world.

Marc Blinder, a creative director for Context Optional, a social media marketing company, explains it like this: "When you want

---

2 Arianna Huffington, "Companies and Causes: Social Media Jumpstart a Marketing
  Revolution," April 6, 2011, *The Huffington Post*
3 "2012: It Was a Very Good Year for Social Giving," December 11th, 2012,
  MDG Advertising Blog

people to know about the good you're doing in the world, Facebook is a prime mobilization platform. People want their friends to see them doing something good – those types of activities are very palatable in this medium because it's a place users expect to be engaged in this way."[4]

As we mentioned at the beginning of this chapter, few people knew anything about the Uganda situation – until they woke up one morning in March of 2012 and suddenly saw *Kony 2012* popping up left and right on all their friends' Facebook walls. Social media is where people like to hear about – and have the opportunity to participate in – doing good in the world. That's why it's the perfect place to tell everyone about your cause.

And actually, it's a pretty good place to do your own Celebrity Brand StorySelling™ as well. In the next chapter, we'll give you some tips and tricks on how best to bring your StorySelling™ to life through tweets, status updates, boards and "shares" - through the primary communication gathering places of our time!

---

4 David Hessekiel, "Cause Marketing on Facebook: Truths, Tips and Trends," November 8th, 2011, *Forbes.com*

CHAPTER 15

STORYSELLING™ WITH SOCIAL MEDIA
Creating (and Controlling) the Conversation

The band was ready to play…but, unfortunately, there were only two people in the theatre.

Alex Hwang, Daniel Chae, John Chong, Jennifer Rim, Sally Kang and Joe Chun were all the children of Korean immigrants – and they had gotten together to start a rock group that they named "Monsters Calling Home," the title reflecting their conflicted nationalities. They were based in L.A. and, of course, were anxious to break into the music business with their unusual approach – a genre they called "gangster Oriental folk."

The first step to success, in their minds, was to produce a music video with the potential to go viral on YouTube.

Only problem? They didn't really have the budget to create anything all that exciting – or even a cool location to just shoot the band performing. They were so broke that, many nights, they didn't have a place to sleep after their club gigs and had to ask people in the audience if they had a place where they could crash.

What they did have, however, was their *cars* – which were a source of amusement to everybody that knew them, because they all drove Hondas. In the words of Hwang, "We always joke that maybe it's because we're all Asian."

So they shot video of themselves playing their various instruments squeezed inside their vehicles – and they then edited it together and posted it on YouTube. And, to their surprise, the video started racking up hits. A lot of them.

So many hits that it reached the attention of Honda's advertising agency. They thought the video was cool and hired the band to put on a special show for six hundred members of Honda's high level management. It felt like it could be the most important night of their band's life.

The band was ready to rock on that magic night – but they were informed that the company had called an emergency meeting. Most of the management couldn't make it to the concert. Which is why they were standing onstage in the theatre Honda had booked, ready to play a full show for the only *two* people who were available to come.

Finally, a Honda representative told them the company was cancelling the show altogether. The band was devastated – until he told them the second piece of news. They never really intended to have the band play for Honda management in the first place. The real gig? Playing for the entire country on ABC's late-night talk show *Jimmy Kimmel Live!*, whose studio just happened to be across the street.

The band's mood quickly changed from despair to joy – and, with absolutely no preparation time, they raced over to Kimmel's studio, where they played their hearts out for their first national audience.

The above incident happened on Tuesday, September 18th, 2012, and was an integral part of Honda's social media campaign, "Honda Loves You Back," which was designed to gain the brand some traction with younger demos and also to create a viral video that would spread across social media like wildfire.

And it worked.

Honda received a ton of "old media" coverage for the Jimmy Kimmel stunt - and their Facebook page currently has two-and-a-half million "Likes."

As we touched on in the last chapter, social media StorySelling™ requires some different techniques than traditional StorySelling™ – but it also can provide a bigger (and more cost-effective) pay-off when successful. In this chapter, we'll talk about how to create a compelling conversation on Facebook, Twitter and other social media outlets – and why it's a necessity, in today's marketplace, to take advantage of these mostly-free and all-powerful tools. We'll also put up some red flags you should avoid when implementing your StorySelling™ in social media

DRIVING SOCIAL MEDIA SUCCESS

When Honda booked Monsters Calling Home on *Jimmy Kimmel Live!*, it wasn't an isolated incident for the carmaker – no, social media has been a must for its overall marketing plan, especially since "Million Mile Joe" became a viral video success story in late 2011. If you're not familiar with Million Mile Joe, his real name is Joe LoCicero, he lives in Maine and he managed to drive his 1990 Honda Accord over a million miles. Honda threw him a parade and gifted him with a brand new Accord when his odometer reached the magic number.

Since then Honda has done numerous other StorySelling™ events through social media, such as:

• Profiling Tim Mings, the last remaining "shadetree" mechanic (a mechanic who fixes cars at his home) who works on the original Honda N600 Hatchback (the first Honda model spe-cifically made for the U.S. market).

• Launching a "Pintermission" campaign on Pinterest by gifting top site users with $500 to bring their Pinterest boards to life.

• Returning the favor when a man mowed a Honda logo into his backyard – by mowing the man's name into the lawn of its corporate headquarters

Now, none of the above efforts have anything to do with directly selling cars – but all of them *do* create an extremely positive conversation about the Honda brand.

John Watts, the American Honda senior manager of digital marketing, gave some insight into the company's strategy at the 2012 Advertising Age Social Engagement conference. "People are valuing kindness over exclusivity in a brand," said Watts, who also added, "Your storytelling must be an extension of your brand. Authenticity is not reality. Authenticity is not testimonials. Authenticity is not a spokesperson, a celebrity who may not even buy your product. Authenticity must be *earned.*"

Let's talk about how you can use StorySelling™ to start earning *your* authenticity.

CONVERSATION STARTERS

In the last chapter, we talked about how social media is perfect for cause marketing, simply because people enjoy being a part of efforts they feel are positive and important, and they can feel like they've done something simply by "sharing" stories about them.

These kinds of causes are, by their very nature, authentic – so cause marketers don't have to worry too much about building trust. Anyone building a Celebrity Brand, however, does. You don't ever want to be seen as a one-note marketer on Facebook or Twitter, where your statuses could be mistaken for spam. Otherwise, you'll lose followers faster than a politician caught taking a bribe.

The way you avoid that situation is by providing value in your social media StorySelling™ – and also not making it all about you. You need to be a combination of *teacher, entertainer* and *benefactor* in everything you do – and most of all, you have to be *interesting*.

That might seem like a tall order, but there are some simple methods you can use to put all those together to work for your brand. Another carmaker closer to home, Ford Motors, also has a robust social media strategy that works – and Ford's head of social media marketing, Scott Monty, shared some valuable advice at the 2013 New Media Expo that is well worth passing on:

- **Let fans tell your story.**
  At first, Ford tried to tell its story to consumers through one-way StorySelling™ – but soon found out it was much more effective to let Ford owners relate how they connect to the brand. What started out as "The Ford Story" became "Ford Social" in 2011 – as the company focused on sharing customer stories rather than relating their own corporate narrative. In the words of Monty, "If you have a good product, let go of your fear and let others tell your story." Real people have authenticity built in, as Honda also proved through its viral successes with Monsters Calling Home and Million Mile Joe.

- **Rethink how you share news.**
  The big car companies usually unveil new models at trade shows – but all that competition means a heated scramble to get the attention of the journalists covering these industry events. In 2011, Ford decided to launch their new Ford Explorer online instead - and primed the pump by engaging some of the brand's most influential fans months ahead of time, by giving them special advance access. Once again, *real people* were creatively utilized to give the brand the authenticity it was after, and to create a viable grassroots strategy. "When you treat amateurs like pros, they tend to act like pros," says Monty.

- **Share content everywhere you can.**
  When Ford created its own web series, "Escape My Life,"

to promote its Escape models, it went well beyond YouTube and posted the videos on Hulu and other platforms to make sure the videos reached the widest possible audience. As most of these outlets are free, why not make sure you're reaching everyone you possibly can? According to Monty, you should **"embrace the platforms your audience is using, not [just] the ones you're comfortable with."**

- **Be willing to experiment and learn from mistakes.**
  Ford put a lot of effort and star power (Ryan Seacrest and "The Soup" star Joel McHale) into a major social media campaign, "Random Acts of Fusion" – but it failed to catch on. Why? Monty thinks it was too complicated – and he left out the all-important factor of using real people to anchor and promote the campaign. However, you still never know what might and might not catch on – so it doesn't hurt to try something (but we suggest doing so in a limited way, at first, to test the waters, since few of us have the resources that Ford has to throw at marketing!).

- **Think long-range.**
  Ford believes in creating an "engagement ladder" that, over time, builds trust and creates authenticity. "Social media is a marriage, not a one-night stand," says Monty. Social media StorySelling™ should always create an ongoing long-range narrative that builds towards higher and higher goals. For example, Honda is continuing its "Honda Loves You Back" campaign by continuing to identify and honor Honda owners who show the brand their devotion in unique and fun ways. One woman sent the company a painting she made of her Honda – and, in return, the company put a portrait of the woman up in their company headquarters!

There are two qualities we want to stress that are almost essential to any social media StorySelling™ – *authenticity* and *user-engagement*, both of which are highly evident in all of the above points. One tends to feed the other; when you find ways to involve your audience in your social media narratives, it can't help but up the authenticity factor. Ryan Seacrest might work gangbusters on *American Idol,* but, when it comes to Facebook, Million Mile Joe just might be the bigger "star" for your brand (and he's a lot more affordable).

SOCIAL MEDIA RED FLAGS

While it's true social media offers almost unlimited opportunities to StorySell your Celebrity Brand, it also contains a lot of hidden dangers as well. Many online business and marketing websites routinely spotlight social media disasters experienced by brands; the major missteps that are revealed are usually ones that could have easily been avoided.

To help you avoid a 'Twitter-astrophe' or an epic Facebook fail, keep these "red flags" in mind as you go about spinning your story on social sites:

• **Red Flag #1: Real time can be a real disaster.**
One of the best things about social media is that you can act, react and interact immediately in real time; that means you can use current events to your advantage and respond to your followers without delay. This, however, can also be the *worst* thing about social media; sometimes you post too quickly without thinking something through.

For example, just as Hurricane Sandy was threatening to bring record-setting devastation to the New York and New Jersey shorelines, American Apparel posted a marketing message saying that "Just in case you're bored during the storm, 20% off everything for the next 36 hours." Customers quickly responded online with some stormy criticism of the company's insensitivity to those in the path of the natural disaster.

As a matter of fact, current events can burn you another way as well…

- **Red Flag #2: Pre-scheduled postings can become a problem.**
Many programs out there allow you to compose your tweets and Facebook postings in advance and schedule when they actually go "live" on the sites. This is an excellent way to map out your StorySelling™ in advance, since you and/or your staff don't have to worry about personally posting at designated times. However, current events can also intrude on this pre-planned process, as the National Rifle Association discovered to its regret. The morning after the tragic shootings at a movie theatre in Aurora, Colorado, the NRA's scheduled tweet chirpily noted, "Good morning, shooters. Happy Friday!"

Whenever a major event hits the headlines, you should immediately double-check to see how the big news might impact what you're planning to post on social media. And if you're unsure, by all means get an outside opinion, because you never want to invite a backlash.

Even though it can be very easy to do just that…

- **Red Flag #3: Your brand weaknesses can come back to bite you.**
Everyone wants to think that the public views their brand in a completely favorable light – but that leads to some dangerous tunnel vision that has already resulted in negative consequences for some of the world's biggest companies.

In 2012, McDonalds paid to promote its restaurants on Twitter with the hashtag #McDStories – intending to do some positive StorySelling™ of its own. Unfortunately, the fast food chain has its detractors out there and they quickly hijacked the hashtag with such devastating tweets as, *"Fingernail in my Big Mac," "Ordered a McDouble, something in the damn thing chipped my molar,"* and *"Hospitalized for food poisoning after eating McDonalds in 1989. Never ate there again and became a Vegetarian. Should have sued."*

The lifespan of this StorySelling™ campaign? Exactly one hour – and then McDonalds yanked the campaign for good.

So be aware of who out there might have it in for you and your brand – and beware of handing over control of your StorySelling™ to everyone and anyone when you proceed. (Also note that Honda, with its Honda Loves You Back campaign, *chose* who they involved in their StorySelling™.)

And speaking of control…

- **Red Flag #4: The wrong person might have access to your social media accounts.**

  "Ryan found two more 4 bottle packs of Midas Touch beer…when we drink, we do it right."

  "I find it ironic that Detroit is known as the Motor City, yet no one around here knows how to f***ing drive."

  "Obamas gma even knew it was going 2be bad. She died 3 days b4 he became president."

Those are three "interesting" tweets, wouldn't you say? What's even more interesting is the fact that they were sent, respectively, by the official accounts of the Red Cross, Chrysler Autos and the KitchenAid appliance company!

Obviously, these were personal tweets that accidentally went out under these brands' banners – but they also took those companies' StorySelling™ efforts in a very weird direction that was undoubtedly offensive to many. Yes, it can be hard to prevent this kind of social media accident – but the first step is to limit the staff members who have access to your brand accounts and make sure they're responsible with that access (not to mention sober!).

But when the worst does happen…

- **Red Flag #5: Damage can spin out of control.**
When your social media StorySelling™ inadvertently leads
to disaster, as it did with McDonalds' twitter campaign, shut
it down as quickly as possible – and consider how to spin a
negative into a positive.

Yes, it is possible to do just that – let's take a look at yet
another automaker to prove it. Toyota found itself trapped
in a negative narrative when a now-defunct blogging site,
MommyNetworks.org, sent out emails claiming that, if anyone spread positive news about Toyota, they could receive
a $10 gift card from Amazon. Suddenly, social media sites
were swarming with accusations that the car manufacturer
was trying to buy good buzz.

Toyota, however, was monitoring all Twitter conversations
in which they were involved – and quickly saw what was
developing. Within hours, they denied having any affilia-
tion with MommyNetworks.org – and their negative buzz
quickly turned positive as their side of the story got out.
They racked up a StorySelling™ win by reacting quickly
and honestly.

You can't always prevent a negative social media experience – but you can control your reaction to it by staying
professional and positive, and staying focused on the good
things about your brand. Never get into the gutter and fight
it out with an opponent – always try and stay above the fray.

Yes, social media has its dangers – and those dangers might
tempt you to opt out of StorySelling™ through social media. We
think that's a mistake – because there are far more advantages
to using Facebook, Twitter, Google+, Pinterest and the like than
not using them, especially since they have become a primary
communication tool for people all around the world. Don't believe us? Well, believe this – if the number of Facebook users
formed a country, it would be the third biggest in the world.

It can be hard to measure the actual benefits you derive from your social media activity – but we think Scott Monty, Ford's social media mastermind who we referred to earlier in this chapter, has the right take on the situation. He says, "What's the ROI of putting your pants on every day? It's hard to measure, but there are negative consequences for not doing it."

Another way to look at it is through a famous quote from Woody Allen: "90% of life is showing up." When you show up on social media, you have the best opportunity available today to directly connect your audience to your StorySelling™ narrative.

After all, if Honda loves its customers back, shouldn't you do the same with yours?

CHAPTER 16

THE NEXT CHAPTER OF YOUR STORYSELLING™
Securing Your Brand for the Future

The singer was washed up.

After twenty years of success, his career was in a giant downward spiral. He no longer had a manager or a record deal; he also had difficulty getting any gigs outside of Las Vegas. His second marriage had just collapsed and, perhaps most ominously, he had an enormous drug problem.

After a near-fatal cocaine overdose, he knew he had to make a change – fast.

He called his son, an aspiring musician himself, and told him that he needed a career makeover. It seemed like nobody wanted to listen to his kind of music anymore - and that what was left of his career was doomed to failure.

The son listened and thought about it. And he finally said to his dad, "Did people stop listening to Beethoven just because his music was old?"

The singer agreed with the point. And the son made plans to connect his father with a whole new generation of listeners.

Suddenly, he was booking his dad on college tours he never would have considered before. He got him appearances on the David Letterman show as well as *The Simpsons.* The singer also found himself in a fashion layout in *SPIN* magazine, as well as performing in L.A. with the Red Hot Chili Peppers.

The plan began to work. The singer was able to make a new deal with his old record company. And the initial record he made under that deal was the very first totally digital album ever to be recorded.

Suddenly, the old singer was in with the younger crowd, who respected both his musical integrity and his willingness to reach out to them. A few years later, he not only had a music video on MTV (when MTV still showed music videos), but he also headlined his own award-winning *MTV Unplugged* episode with such unlikely guests as Elvis Costello. His sales skyrocketed with the new generation and his peers continued to recognize his new phase of artistic excellence by awarding him numerous Grammys, including the organization's highest award, Album of the Year.

Tony Bennett, now 86 years old, is the oldest person to ever appear on the *Billboard Top 100,* thanks to his successful 2011 release of *Duets II.* He is still in demand all over the world and he has no plans to retire.

And he is still managed by his son Danny, who, in 2012, produced a branded film for Tony entitled *The Zen of Bennett.*

YOUR STORYSELLING™ DOESN'T HAVE TO HAVE AN ENDING

Remember when everyone carried a Blackberry? Remember when Nokia was the leader in cell phones? Or when everyone signed on to the Internet through America Online (which was actually huge enough to briefly take over Time-Warner)?

These giant brands, that seemed unstoppable at one time, are now on the ropes.

Here's the horrifying truth: Every brand, no matter how successful in its time, has a built-in expiration date – *unless they take the necessary action to keep their StorySelling™ narrative relevant and alive.*

Danny Bennett took that action on behalf of his father; he took someone who was widely thought to be a dinosaur in modern music and made him matter again – and he did this through a three-pronged approach that paid huge dividends:

- He continued Tony Bennett's commitment to the kind of music and performance that brought him his initial fame and public good will.

- He widened Bennett's exposure to a whole new audience without watering down his music.

- He positioned his father as a pioneer in the changing technology of the music business, so he would never be left behind again.

It was enough to cement Bennett's place in show business for the rest of his life. Otherwise, he might have wound up forgotten and broke, like so many others of his generation. As of this writing, however, he is still releasing albums, doing concerts and making TV appearances.

The tragedy of a successful brand gone bad is that it's hard enough to establish one in the first place - so why let all that hard work go to waste? It's kind of like a mountain climber who's made it through sheer force of will to the top of an incredible peak - only to fall to his death down the other side.

But it doesn't have to be that way. In this chapter, we're going to discuss how you can keep your StorySelling™ alive – by protecting, nurturing and progressing your brand story so that it stays fresh and relevant for years to come.

But first...how do you know if your Celebrity Brand is beginning to lose traction – and might be headed downhill?

WHEN YOUR STORYSELLING™ STALLS

The first step to fixing a problem, as any self-help group will tell you, is to recognize that you have one: Your Celebrity Brand is no different. Here are a few simple ways to detect if your brand's StorySelling™ isn't packing the same narrative punch it used to:

- **Your Sales Are Down**
  We would venture a guess and say this is probably THE most obvious sign of a StorySelling™ problem (unless there are other external forces at work driving down your revenues). If less people are buying what you're selling, less people are receptive to your messaging. Your brand story isn't connecting like it should anymore – and you need to determine why that is.

- **Your Client List Is Shrinking or Segmenting**
  Fox News often boasts about how it's the number one cable news channel – but one big red alert they should be paying attention to is that, even though their audience is the largest, it's also the *oldest*, with a median viewer age of 65. That means that they, just like Tony Bennett did in 1979, might wake up one day to find that their audience is quickly vanishing.

  Sometimes you can still be making the money you want and ignore the fact that you're not getting enough new clients in through the door. You want to continue to serve whatever niche you're succeeding with – but you also want to make sure you're growing beyond that niche, not shrinking with it.

- **You've Forgotten Your Own Success Story**
  Success can sometimes disconnect you from your roots and cause you to dismiss or not recall why your clients were attracted to you in the first place. The StorySelling™ narrative which first successfully broke out your brand should still be

in play – as Tony Bennett's son was smart enough to realize. He simply changed Tony's approach to the marketplace to *build* on his existing narrative, not rewrite it.

• **You're Too Much About Yourself**

Success can also cause you to be too wrapped up in yourself and ignore your potential customers' needs. When that happens, your StorySelling™ can end up focusing too much on you and not enough on those who might buy from you. When Tony Bennett's career was on the rocks, he wasn't focused on how to change things up for a new generation, he most likely was wondering why his past success didn't simply magically continue. It was up to Danny Bennett to really look for the first time at the potential untapped market for his dad's music.

• **You're Too Comfortable**

In many cases, all of the above signs of brand fatigue come from this last red alert: Because your brand is doing very well, you grow extremely comfortable and you take your eye off the ball. That's when the strikes start flying past you.

When you get locked into a certain way of running your business, as Tony Bennett did, with no attempt to change your StorySelling™ with the times or the marketplace, decay is inevitable. As we said earlier, every brand has a built-in expiration date – unless you do something about it.

So – what is that something that you should do? Don't worry, as usual, we have some suggestions…

HOW DO YOU KEEP THE MUSIC PLAYING?

The above question comes from the title of one of the many standards that Tony Bennett is still singing as of this writing. In this section, we're going to use a few other titles from Tony's best-selling songs and albums to illustrate some proven ways you can ensure long-term brand success – and keep your StorySelling™ humming even through changing times. We'll also provide the questions you should ask yourself to stimulate a new perspective on your Celebrity Brand.

TONY TIP #1:
"IT HAD TO BE YOU"

There is a reason a brand becomes successful in the first place. And the worst thing you can do is pretend that reason never existed.

Tony Bennett's career slide actually began in the late sixties, as rock n' roll began to totally dominate the charts and radio play. It was such a difficult climate that even Frank Sinatra ended up retiring for a couple of years. As for Tony, his record label was demanding he record the new Top 40 rock songs in an effort to make him appear "hip." That resulted in a record album entitled *Tony Sings the Great Hits of Today,* featuring a groovy far-out illustration of Tony with swinging striped bell-bottoms and a floral ascot.

As you might guess, it turned out nobody really wanted to hear Tony Bennett sing "Eleanor Rigby" – or, for that matter, see him in those pants.

When we say, "It Had to Be You," what we really mean is "It HAS to Be You." If you try to change your brand story too much in an attempt to stay current, you'll lose your old clients – and probably not pick up many new ones, as you'll be regarded as an inauthentic pretender to those who weren't already customers.

The biggest brands in the world have made the mistake of ignoring what made them big in the first place. For those of you who don't remember it, in 1985, Coca-Cola was in a panic. Pepsi was nipping at the soft drink giant's heels and Coke thought it had to change – radically. So, in an effort to make Coke more like Pepsi, the company suddenly began selling "New Coke."

Expert marketers to this day cite the move as one of the worst marketing blunders ever made, because New Coke provoked a huge consumer backlash. The original Coca Cola had been a mainstay of people's lives - and they felt betrayed that a long-time tradition had suddenly been snatched away from them. The haters became so vocal that Coke had to backtrack: They first began selling what they now called "Classic Coke" side-by-side with New Coke on supermarket shelves, until New Coke quietly went away for good.

Coke's incredible StorySelling™ began with…well, Coke. And by abruptly changing their core product, they almost ended that story. Tony Bennett endured by remaining Tony Bennett, not try-ing to be New Tony Bennett. The lesson? Be who you are – there are other things you can change (that we're about to discuss).

Ask Yourself: What StorySelling™ elements do you absolutely need to keep in place? List them and make sure they remain a part of your brand – ALWAYS.

TONY TIP #2:
"STEPPIN' OUT"

We've detailed how Tony's son Danny went out and found a whole new audience for his father (while still maintaining his dad's integrity). Any successful Celebrity Brand should always have this kind of mindset and look for ways of "Steppin' Out" in order to expand their customer list beyond their current crowd (but, again, without diluting their core stories).

For example, Proctor & Gamble's perennial brand, Ivory Soap, was languishing a few years ago. It was known as being a pure, unscented soap in an age where specialty soaps and bath prod-ucts were increasingly popular.

The Great Recession of 2008 inspired a new kind of thinking: the company's research showed that families wanted to be more frugal – and didn't want to buy a different kind of soap for every single family member. That was an opportunity for Ivory, since the soap was suitable for anyone – it was as plain a soap as any-one sold, but with a more powerful brand that the rest.

Kevin Hochman, general manager of Ivory's marketing team, explained to *Forbes,* "From our consumer research, people want to get back to things they know work, and a lot of people have memories of Ivory. We still sell millions of bars of Ivory in the U.S., but there are lots of people who had stopped using Ivory. But there are lots of latent memories in terms of what it means for them and their family. We talked to our retailers; certainly that led us to a reason to believe that if we launched [the advertising] in a certain way we'd have success."[1]

In that advertising, they tapped into Ivory's basic StorySelling™ strength – while going after an entire new generation – and that included Facebook ads that successfully gave Ivory a facelift while keeping it "99 and 44/100% Pure" (as their old slogan used to state).

Ask Yourself: How can you tell your story to a whole new group of potential leads in a way that will appeal to them? What current trends and economic situations might cause your core brand to be appreciated in a way it hadn't been before?

TONY TIP #3:
"DUETS"

In the 2000's, Danny took the Tony Bennett brand to a new level of popularity with a series of "Duets" albums, that featured the veteran singer in harmony with such top contemporary performers as Lady GaGa, Mariah Carey and Carrie Underwood. Of course, this wasn't an original idea (Sinatra had actually pioneered the formula with his last two best-selling albums, *Duets* and *Duets II* in the 1990's), but it was a smart idea – as Bennett gained exposure to the younger fans of those top performers.

In branding circles, this is known as "Co-Branding" – a concept by which you combine your brand with another equally strong brand to gain entrée to each other's customers.

---

1 Jennifer Rooney, "In Ivory Brand Refresh, A Lesson In Going Back To Basics," *Forbes,* January 9, 2012

Examples of this practice abound. For example, in the film *Skyfall*, James Bond drank Heineken beer instead of his traditional vodka martini - because the beer manufacturer thought it was worth paying the producers $45 million to brand their brew with Bond's. On the retail front, you can find at your local supermarket such co-branding products as Lay's Potato Chips with KC Masterpiece barbeque sauce taste, Hershey candy in Breyer's ice cream, and even a Kellogg's Cinnabon breakfast cereal.

You can do your own co-branding duet either on an individual project or a joint venture – but be careful when you pick who your partner is going to be, to make sure it's not a brand that's going to conflict with your narrative. Many James Bond fans complained in advance about their superspy hero having a brew instead of a mixed drink, since it violated the Bond brand – but the film handled the product placement discretely, trumpeting the 007 connection in its commercials instead.

Ask Yourself: What company or which other type of personal brand might provide a powerful co-branding boost? Who has the type of audience I want to reach – and haven't been able up to now? Would they be a suitable fit for my brand story?

TONY TIP #4:
"I WANNA BE AROUND"

You want your Celebrity Brand to endure – but you're aware that times change and your StorySelling™ needs to change along with it. You're singing "I Wanna Be Around" – but you definitely don't want to be around if it means becoming your version of Tony Bennett in bellbottoms. How do you stay contemporary without losing your identity?

The answer is actually pretty simple – you focus on updating the things that make sense and keep the rest intact. Call it "Concession without Compromise."

For instance, L.L. Bean is a durable brand that has lasted over a century – and one of its signature products over the past 100 years is their popular "Bean Boot." It still looks like the same boot as it was in 1912...and yet it's not. James L. Witherell, who wrote the recent best-seller, *L.L. Bean: The Man and His Company*, explained to *The New York Times* just how the company kept things current without sacrificing their brand story: "About 10 years ago, they completely redesigned, modernized and updated the boot. The material is now better, it's more comfortable, it lasts longer. But what was important to them was that *it look exactly the same as it always has.*"[2] (Italics are ours.)

In other words, L.L. Bean understood their customers wanted to feel as though the company's products were the same – but, at the same time, also wanted them *improved* and up to current standards, as contradictory as that sounds.

One more example of how you stay the same – without getting left behind. A frozen yogurt place named The Bigg Chill has been in operation in Westwood, Los Angeles (near the UCLA campus) for over twenty years – and, on most nights of the week, they still have a line of people waiting to be served that extends out the door.

A few years ago, however, the rise of the new tart yogurt chain, Pinkberry, briefly took a bite out of their sales. The management thought about changing their décor, which favored warm 80's-style colors, to the more pristine white interiors of the new fro-yo success stories – but finally realized they didn't want to change their identity. Instead, they spent a few months creating a "Chill Berry" flavor, designed to compete directly with Pinkberry, and promoted it. They kept their core story intact – and offered an extra competitive product that helped them survive the brief assault on their customer base.

Remember – when Tony Bennett came back, he was the first performer to use the new digital recording technology. Just because you're a brand with some history doesn't mean you have to become history.

---

2 Nicole LaPorte, "A Brand Keeps Its Cool (and Endures)," *The New York Times*, September 3, 2011

Ask Yourself: What aspects of your Celebrity Brand can you update without injuring your core story? What current technology or trend can you tap into in order to remain as competitive as possible?

TONY TIP #5:
"THEY CAN'T TAKE THAT AWAY FROM ME"

Finally, a great way to rekindle interest in your brand is to simply retell your main StorySelling™ narrative in a new and compelling way. Your point of difference from your competitors is something they can't take away from you – so help your customers and clients rediscover what's great about you.

Now, that may involve you rediscovering that greatness in yourself. It may be a matter of you simply doing what you do best again – and re-engaging the marketplace with what made you memorable in the first place, as Tony Bennett did with his carefully-orchestrated career rebirth.

Here's how one company tapped into its history (as well as the country's) to make a significant impact: In 2012, Chrysler, emerging from its recession-era difficulties, bought time during the Super Bowl to run a commercial, narrated by the equally-iconic Clint Eastwood, talking directly about America – and, by implication, Chrysler – returning to greatness. It was a dramatic two minute ad that stirred up some political controversy, but still did the job and got great reviews.

Whatever your core story is about, if it worked once, chances are it will work again. Did anyone ever expect Polaroid cameras to come back? The company bottomed out in bankruptcy court twice since the year 2000, as the age of digital pictures seemed to render its main selling point, photos that instantly develop by themselves, moot.

Now, however, the brand is resurging, simply because the company has found ways to work with other businesses in order to cash in on Polaroid nostalgia (which, ironically, seems to be most appealing to the millennial generation).

"What comes around, goes around" is an expression that can mean good things for any Celebrity Brand – because, even if your brand is facing difficulties, you probably still have the means at your disposal to make a profitable comeback.

Ask Yourself: How does your StorySelling™ narrative connect to your potential customers of today? How can you reframe your story in a compelling way for a new generation – or a totally new market?

We sincerely hope this book has fully communicated how important the concept of StorySelling™ is to any brand, whether it be a Celebrity Brand or that of a company, product or service. When you put forward the right story, you engage the public on a level that your competition can't match, you position yourself in an unforgettable way, and you create the foundation for ongoing success.

Have faith in your StorySelling™ – have faith in your narrative – and you'll discover, as Tony Bennett did, that "The Best Is Yet to Come."

About Nick

An Emmy-Award-Winning Director and Producer, Nick Nanton, Esq. is known as the Top Agent to Celebrity Experts around the world for his role in developing and marketing business and professional experts through personal branding, media, marketing and PR. Nick is recognized as the nation's leading expert on personal branding as Fast Company Magazine's Expert Blogger on the subject and lectures regularly on the topic at major universities around the world. His book *Celebrity Branding You®*, while an easy and informative read, has also been used as a text book at the University level.

The CEO and Chief StoryTeller at The Dicks + Nanton Celebrity Branding Agency, an international agency with more than 1800 clients in 33 countries, Nick is an award-winning director, producer and songwriter who has worked on everything from large scale events to television shows – with the likes of Steve Forbes, Brian Tracy, Jack Canfield (*The Secret*, Creator of the *Chicken Soup for the Soul* Series), Michael E. Gerber, Tom Hopkins, Dan Kennedy and many more.

Nick is recognized as one of the top thought-leaders in the business world and has co-authored 26 best-selling books alongside Brian Tracy, Jack Canfield, Dan Kennedy, Dr. Ivan Misner (Founder of BNI), Jay Conrad Levinson (Author of the Guerilla Marketing Series), Super Agent Leigh Steinberg and many others, including the breakthrough hit *Celebrity Branding You!®*.

Nick has led the marketing and PR campaigns that have driven more than 1000 authors to Best-Seller status. Nick has been seen in *USA Today, The Wall St. Journal, Newsweek, BusinessWeek, Inc. Magazine, The New York Times, Entrepreneur® Magazine, Forbes*, FastCompany.com and has appeared on ABC, NBC, CBS, and FOX television affiliates around the country, as well as CNN, FOX News, CNBC, and MSNBC from coast to coast.

Nick is a member of the Florida Bar, holds a JD from the University Of Floida Levin College Of Law, as well as a BSBA in Finance from the University of Florida's Warrington College of Business. Nick is a voting member of The National Academy of Recording Arts & Sciences (NARAS, Home to The

GRAMMYs), a member of The National Academy of Television Arts & Sciences (Home to the Emmy Awards), co-founder of the National Academy of Best-Selling Authors, a 16-time Telly Award winner, and spends his spare time working with Young Life, Downtown Credo Orlando, Entrepreneurs International and rooting for the Florida Gators with his wife Kristina, and their three children, Brock, Bowen and Addison.

About JW

JW Dicks, Esq. is America's foremost authority on using personal branding for business development. He has created some of the most successful brand and marketing campaigns for business and professional clients to make them the credible celebrity experts in their field and build multi-million dollar businesses using their recognized status.

JW Dicks has started, bought, built, and sold a large number of businesses over his 39-year career and developed a loyal international following as a business attorney, author, speaker, consultant, and business experts' coach. He not only practices what he preaches by using his strategies to build his own businesses, he also applies those same concepts to help clients grow their business or professional practice the ways he does.

JW has been extensively quoted in such national media as *USA Today, The Wall Street Journal, Newsweek, Inc.,* Forbes.com, CNBC.com, and *Fortune Small Business*. His television appearances include ABC, NBC, CBS and FOX affiliate stations around the country. He is the resident branding expert for *Fast Company*'s internationally syndicated blog and is the publisher of *Celebrity Expert Insider*, a monthly newsletter targeting business and brand building strategies.

JW has written over 22 books, including numerous best-sellers, and has been inducted into the National Academy of Best-Selling Authors®. JW is married to Linda, his wife of 42 years, and they have two daughters, two granddaughters and two Yorkies. JW is a 6th generation Floridian and splits his time between his home in Orlando and a beach house on the Florida west coast.

MORE CELEBRITY BRANDING® FOR YOU!

Just as those of you who are successful in life and in business know that you can't expect to stay at the top of your industry if you relax once you reach the pinnacle of success, we also know that you will need to stay on top of your Celebrity Branding® process. In order to make this easy for you, we've created www.DNAgency.com so you can keep up with all the newest tips and strategies that we uncover as we continue to work with some of the biggest and best Experts in business.

Be sure to visit www.DNAgency.com to sign up for our free CelebrityZine™ as well as to find many great resources that you can use so you won't be left behind. We look forward to hearing about your success and welcome your correspondence.

We can be reached at:
Info@DNAgency.com
(800) 980-1626

THE
DICKS + NANTON
CELEBRITY
BRANDING AGENCY®
RESOURCES

BECOME THE RECOGNIZED CELEBRITY EXPERT® IN YOUR FIELD!

A CELEBRITY EXPERT® IS A MASTER IN THE ART OF LIVING

"A master in the art of living draws no sharp distinction between his work and his play, his mind and his body, his education and his recreation. He hardly knows which is which. He simply pursues his vision or excellence through whatever he is doing and leaves others to determine whether he is working or playing. To himself, he always seems to be doing both."

~ James A. Michener

This year has seen the Dicks + Nanton Celebrity Branding Agency®, as well as our clients live that very statement, from beginning the year with 40 amazing clients and their spouses and friends at the 2012 Grammy Awards placing bets with Dan Kennedy at the Kentucky Derby to shooting documentaries at LSU baseball games and in State Governors' homes. We have introduced new legends to our group of Celebrity Experts® like Jack Canfield and Tom Hopkins and will release two new books with our friend and mentor, Brian Tracy.

Inside the pages of your *Celebrity Expert® Insider Special Edition* is a look into not just our world and the things we do to help over a thousand Celebrity Experts® in 26 countries but at how Dicks + Nanton Celebrity Branding Agency® can change both your business and your life. Steak dinners transition into Red Carpet premiers. Tri-fold brochures become shock-and- awe packages that win you business time and time again from your strongest competition who just don't get it. Websites become living, breathing parts of your business that attract the part of your market that is ready to take action with you today. And, yes, your life will forever be changed once you add the irreplaceable title of Best-Selling Author to your arsenal.

So take a look, dream, imagine and live out the words that James A. Michener wrote above. Once you do, your life will never be the same.

Nick, Jack, Lindsay and Greg
The Dicks + Nanton Celebrity Branding Agency®

BE SEEN ON ABC, NBC, CBS AND FOX AFFILIATES ACROSS THE COUNTRY

One thing that separates our Agency from other Media, Marketing or PR films is that we guarantee our results.

And we also guarantee that you will have a great time in the process. Every year we host 6 to 9 of our own branded TV Shows across the country to highlight and

tell your story. From the "Brian Tracy Show" to "The New Masters of Real Estate," "Health and Wellness Today" and "America's PremierExperts®," we have shows that suit every entrepreneur, professional small business owner, author or expert. Appearances on these shows position you as both an expert and a thought leader in your field.

Our TV shoots are unlike any event you have ever attended. From the atmosphere to the media training, from the professional photo shoot to the three-camera live interview, this experience is one you will remember for the rest of your life. Every detail is taken care of for you, from preparation to editing, from makeup to giving you the media credentials that would take a lifetime to get on your own. In addition, you will receive press releases, a hi-def copy of your interview, and more than 50 ways to use the video, the logos and the credibility in your business to get your story, your passion and your emotion into the hands of more people than ever before.

Our next TV season is casting now, and the only way to guarantee yourself media placement on the biggest networks on the planet is to call your Business Agent® at **888-592-0062** today. We look forward to seeing you on set!

BECOME A BEST-SELLING AUTHOR

Once you become a client of the Dicks + Nanton Celebrity Branding Agency®, our singular goal in business is to help you become a Celebrity Expert® in your marketplace. The most effective way to do that is to become a published author, and even better yet, a Best-Selling Author. As an agency client, we will get you signed to a publishing contract with

CelebrityPress® Publishing to work on your own book or join one of our multi-author books with other Celebrity Experts®.

Over the past five years we have helped over 800 clients from all over the world not only become published authors but also elevated their status to Best-Selling Author. We guarantee we can do it for you too!

Over the past year we have given our clients the opportunity to co-author books with legends such as Brian Tracy, Tom Hopkins, Jack Canfield, Dan Kennedy, Michael E. Gerber, Dr. Ivan Misner, Mari Smith and others. Writing, releasing and including these books in your marketing is the most powerful way to develop yourself into a Celebrity Expert® and position yourself as the go-to person in your field.

If you are looking to become a published author of your own book or with other co-authors, speak with one of our Business Agents® today to talk about how we can guarantee your book is a Best-Seller and you become a Best-Selling Author!

Call **888- 592-0062** today and speak with your Business Agent®.

THE NATIONAL ACADEMY OF BEST-SELLING AUTHORS®

Writing a book is one of the greatest ways to give back. Taking that book and marketing it to the world so that it becomes a Best-Seller creates an impact and positions you as a thought leader in your field. In 2010, Nick and JW launched the National Academy of Best-Selling Authors® to recognize and honor the works of authors who have achieved Best-Seller status.

The Academy has inducted over 800 authors, including legends such as Brian Tracy, Michael E. Gerber, Jack Canfield and entrepreneurs and experts just like you who have reached the monumental status of Best-Selling Author!

As part of the National Academy of Best-Selling Authors®, we hold an annual event, The Best-Seller's Summit and Golden Gala Awards to recognize the accomplishments of Best-Selling Authors. In 2012, we were honored to present the 3rd annual Best-Seller's Summit and Golden

Gala Awards right in the heart of Hollywood at the historic Roosevelt Hotel, the site of the first Academy Awards.

Every year we gather Best-Selling Authors from across the world to award them our Quilly Statue, which is made by the same group that produces the Oscars and the Grammy Awards!

The event is an opportunity to learn from the world's top thought leaders and join in a celebration of entrepreneurship and authorship with a group of peers who have elevated their status to Best-Selling Author.

If you are a Best-Selling Author or become one with our help, you will be invited to a once-in-a-lifetime Red Carpet experience to recognize your accomplishments. Reserve your seat now or get pre-registered for our 2013 event by speaking with your Business Agent® today.

BIGPRINT® MEDIA EXPOSURE

What you do in your business and how you help your clients is a story worth telling the world about. In our BigPrint® Media Campaigns, we help you do just that and place your story in major media publications as well as hundreds of dot-coms across the web.

I'm sure you have heard the expression "content is King" when it comes to marketing your business online. In our BigPrint® Packages, we help you create content that is extremely valuable, developing links back to your website and bringing you media credibility in the process.

Our team of expert writers begin by interviewing you and crafting a core story about you and your business. This is a big-time feature article and is a story that you can use well after this campaign ends. The story is then syndicated online, and we get a quote, link and image from you to place in one of the print media we are working with, from *USA Today*, to *The Wall Street Journal* or even *Inc. Magazine*.

Many of our clients frame the "tear sheets" that run in these publications and have them hanging in their offices in recognition of their appearance.

Additionally, every month our team will follow up with you to write press releases about you and your business to syndicate online, again creating more and more content for you. This package is truly the symbol of using media, marketing and PR together to grow your business.

Contact your Business Agent® today at **888-592-0062** to see how you can join us in an opportunity to showcase you in our next BigPrint® Campaign!

THE CELEBRITY EXPERT®
MASTERMIND EXPERIENCE

Napoleon Hill famously wrote in his classic book *Think and Grow Rich*:

> *"Economic advantages may be created by any person who surrounds himself with the advice, counsel, and personal cooperation of a group of men who are willing to lend him wholehearted aid, in a spirit of PERFECT HARMONY. This form of cooperative alliance has been the basis of nearly every great fortune. Your understanding of this great truth may definitely determine your financial status."*

We have found this statement to be true in our own business. It is why we continually surround ourselves with coaches, experts and mentors like Brian Tracy or Dan Kennedy. It's why we continually go to events all over the world to learn, meet new people and engage in new experiences.

The Celebrity Expert® Mastermind experiences, however, are unlike anything you have ever been a part of!

• Have you ever ridden a scooter around the island of Bermuda while talking about your marketing materials?

• What about getting your expansion ideas heard and assessed by lawyers, doctors, consultants and our Executive Team?

- Have you closed a deal while listening to Paul McCartney or Bruce Springsteen at the Grammy Awards?
- We have even created lifelong partnerships and friendships while betting on funny horse names at the Kentucky Derby.

In the past two years, we have taken an exclusive group of Celebrity Experts® with us to work, engage, open up, come clean, and leave with clarity and inspiration to how they are going to live out the life of a Celebrity Expert®. We come together in formal meetings, take notes and consume ideas until our hands are tired and our brains cannot take anymore.

Our Mastermind programs are small-group experiences unlike any other and are limited. If you would like to apply to join this exclusive group that travels and learns in some of the most fun locations in the world, please email **info@dnagency.com** today or call your Business Agent® at **888-592-0062**

LET US BUILD YOUR DIGITAL DNA

What happens when a customer or prospect Googles your name or the name of your business? Do you like the results? Would you like to own those results like a true Celebrity Expert®? Online Marketing Expert Lindsay Dicks has developed online branding, content and website strategies for hundreds of Celebrity Experts® across the world, and you could be next.

Today, your "credibility" is based on what appears in search engine results. And, unfortunately, not having any results (or just your website) can be just as damaging as bad results because you are invisible to your prospects.

We understand that in today's online world, your web presence is much more than just a website (although, you better have one of those, too!). Your online brand is EVERY piece of content out there on the internet. Our proven system not only showcases your expert status and dominates the search engine results, but it will help you suppress any negative listings you may have that are hurting you.

Our Digital DNA Packages range from website design to total turnkey online marketing systems and are priced according to your needs.

• Custom website design

• Content writing services with search engine optimization

• Blog writing and syndication

• Press release writing and syndication

• Social media marketing

• Micro-sites

• Link building

• And more

To see how you stack up with your Digital DNA and to finally create a website that attracts business and brings new prospects into your sales funnel, request a website and online marketing review today by calling us at **800-989-5690** or contacting Lindsay at **info@CelebritySites.com**.

A FULL DOCUMENTARY FILM PRODUCTION... STARRING YOU!

Nothing captivates someone quite like a movie. It's why we have been spending Friday and Saturday nights eating popcorn, drinking soda pop, and watching movies on the big screen since 1896!

Coming from his entertainment background, Nick always dreamed of producing a feature film. And it just so happened that a great group of clients were not only able to finance his first film with him, but they helped him earn an Emmy for Best Director along the way.

That first film was "Jacob's Turn," a story about a 4-year-old boy with Down Syndrome playing in his first baseball game. The documentary was released in 2010 and earned Nick an Emmy for Director. Since then, Nick and the entire Agency have caught movie fever. In 2011, Celebrity Films released "Car Men," a documentary about used-car dealer Tracy Myers. The film has been a game changer for both Nick and Tracy, and a new way of telling stories about businesses through film was born.

In fact, the documentaries have become a movement, with over 10 clients signed for the upcoming months, including a new series on the Biography Channel called "Profiles of Success®."

The Celebrity Films experience is a full 2-day shoot full of excitement and anticipation for you, your staff and everyone in your community. Words cannot do justice to the impact that these films can have on your business, from throwing local movie screenings for all your clients at a rented-out theater to being featured on "Profiles of Success" on the Biography Channel.

To see the latest film trailer and to schedule an appointment to talk about creating a film about your business, please visit: **www.CelebrityFilms.com.**

MARKET YOURSELF LIKE A CELEBRITY EXPERT®

Over the past five years, we have not only helped over 1,500 clients become Celebrity Experts® through media, marketing and PR, but we have also developed the best products and processes to market Celebrity Experts® to their target market.

For the first time ever, we are opening up our marketing team to you. Not only are we bringing you the best media, marketing and PR opportunities outlined in this catalog, but we are going to help you use each and every piece

and create a turnkey marketing campaign to attract your home-run clients, close more business, and truly become the definitive Celebrity Expert® in your marketplace. This unique marketing process is broken down into 6 steps which comprise the Celebrity Expert® Marketing System.

Step 1: Your Business and Marketing Assessment

Step 2: Lead Capturing and Database Management

Step 3: New Client acquisition

Step 4: Client retention and referral based Marketing

You are no longer guessing, Hoping or Stringing Pieces together

The best part of the Celebrity Expert® Marketing System is that we do everything for you. From content creation to copywriting, list management and sequencing, we will build a marketing process and system just like ours but custom tailored for you and your market.

Best yet, for a limited time, you can lock in your own exclusive territory for us to work with just you in your business niche and market. Imagine taking our proven Celebrity Expert® Marketing System, having it run your marketing, and at the same time keeping out your competition.

Get started by giving our CMO, Greg Rollett, a call at: **888-592-0062** or email him at **greg@dnagency.com**.

WHAT OTHERS ARE SAYING ABOUT THE *STORYSELLING:*

"I love working with Nick and his team. They can absolutely help you get to the next level. Nick does everything he promises and then some!"

– Jack Canfield

It's not just what we receive – all you promised and more – it's that you actually get it done and get it done fast. Usually, companies have an offer and the client (at least in my past experience) has to do all the work…even when they don't understand what the work is. So, the client has to almost learn your industry to understand what they need to do. And when they fall short and miss deadlines, it's like, "…oh well, clients fault…thanks for the money." You help walk through it and you follow up. I missed an email once – I don't know how – but then I got a call. Your staff is very nice and supportive, and even when I was a pain in the ### and wanted my picture changed and a comma placed, not once did I get a scoff or a scolding. It made me want to help and protect your staff and at least give them huge thanks for how they helped me. It was really "aggrevation-less". Is that a word? I learned so much through them, it was really fun. I was nervous but they weren't and now I'm not either. I previously thought…

if I hire a company to do thing,s they create a lot more work for me. But it wasn't that way with you guys. I could just go on forever. The Gala was spectacular and fun too. Your company is the best company I have ever worked with! I have had several company relationships in the past 25 years that were good, but your company inspired me!

– Rebecca Gail Barcy

Emmy award winning public relations expert Nick Nanton has done an outstanding job propelling me into the spotlight. Using his proven strategies and track record for success he has in a short time not only made me a best selling author through an excellent book deal he has also made me the Bankruptcy Expert Blogger at FastCompany. I highly recommend Nick and his agency to anyone who needs a great public relations strategy!

– Alex Wathen, Esq

Many people in business today are quick to make promises but fall far short when it comes to delivering. Nick Nanton is a guy that makes big promises and gets the job done! He is a master at what he does and will help move you to the next level in your profession. He is a guy that you need to get on your team! I am thrilled at what he did for me and he will certainly be my go to guy in the future! Thanks Nick for being the pro that you are and for moving me to the next level!

– Richard P. Hastings, Esq.

Thank you Nick for the opportunity and FANTASTIC follow through of your team! It was an awesome experience to have participated in.

– Camille Scielzi

Not only is Nick a great guy, he's a great business partner as well. He's the top agent for celebrity speakers like myself. He helps us get better known so that we can charge more money and charge it more often.

He's also worked with great friends of mine like Dan Kennedy, Jeff Walker, Mari Smith and Ron LeGrand along with many, many more. What he does, is he helps you to maximize your brand and your income by making people see you as special, different and more valuable than your competitors. He's also known for helping experts create a platform and elevating them to celebrity expert status in their fields.

We see people you've never heard of before that one year later they're considered to be the 'go to' person on a particular subject. They get interviewed on radio, television, newspapers even though you've never heard of them before and it's all done by Nick Nanton. He's the best in the world at what he does and he's one of the most high integrity guys myself and my team have ever worked with. If you're looking for an agent to maximize your celebrity status, your business and your income Nick is your guy. Nick is our guy.

– Brian Tracy

Yesterday I had a consulting engagement with Jack and Nick. It was the most unbelievable experience. Before my consulting session, I was a little apprehensive as many of us are when we think about hiring coaches or consultants. I was wondering, "What am I going to get? Am I going to get what I expect? Is it going to be worth my time, value?" Well I'm here to tell you that the answer to all of those questions is YES, and I got tons of value.

I can't even put into words what I walked out of that room with yesterday. I had an expectation. I had a goal of what I wanted to receive from that session. It was exponentially worth more than what I paid. Wherever you're at in your career, whatever you're thinking about working on, whether it's improving your celebrity status, or improving your business these are the guys to work with. Don't worry about the cost, make the call, get booked, work with them today and it will positively impact your business and your life more than you can possibly expect.

– Kenny Chapman

Peter Howley, Chairman of The Howley Management Group works with CEOs to turn great ideas into great business. Now, by utilizing our trademark Media, Marketing and PR strategies, Peter has turned his own ideas into great business! Following a feature story and press release we syndicated introducing Peter Howley as one of America's PremierExperts® Trendsetters in the New Economy, Peter was invited to speak at a Webinar from Singapore on "Web 3.0 and Mobility Innovation in Asia". His speech during the Webinar then led to an invitation to a speaking engagement in January 2012. By utilizing our media tools and public relations services, Peter has been able to expand his brand and rise above his peers. Great job, Peter and Congrats on your success!

– Peter Howley

"I joined the Ultimate Celebrity Branding Experience® for three specific reasons. 1) To become the leading authority in the US on vacation homes. 2) To be able to walk away with a book, a TV show and other materials I can use in my marketing efforts in the future. 3) To learn more about what I must do to grow my businesses; Florida Leisure Vacation Homes, Total Real Estate Solutions and www.GoCruisePlanner.com.

Nick promised me that he would deliver on all three counts and that I would have a great time doing so. At the time I was a little skeptical but I took the plunge and twelve months later, I can honestly say it has been one of the best business decisions I have ever made. Not only have I had a blast as we visited Orlando, Hollywood and New York, but I have learned so much more than I had envisioned and have improved the revenue and profitability of my business.

Nick has way over delivered on what he promised and I have absolutely no hesitation in saying to other business owners out there, that this is a "MUST DO" and as anyone who knows me will tell you...I don't use those words lightly. Thanks to Nick and his team...it's been fantastic."

– Nigel Worrall

"Hi this is Kimberlee Frank "The Real Estate Junkie" and I am writing to let you know how joining America's PremierExperts® made a difference in my life. First off, I have shared the stage with a lot of people. However, it was always me having to impress my audience. Now, thanks to America›s PremierExperts®, I have a long list of credentials that allows me to get on any stage. The media coverage was out of this world. The friendship with Jack, Nick, and Lindsay is something that can not be replaced, we will always be connected. I have written many courses and wanted to write a book but never seemed to find time. With the help of America's PremierExperts®, they made it happen and not in years but everything was done in just 12 months. I just wanted to say "Thanks". I couldn,t have gotten this type of media coverage, book, and articles without your help. I would recommend this experience to anyone who is seriously looking to build their creditability fast!

– Kimberlee Frank

"Participating in the Ultimate Celebrity Branding Experience® was the perfect launching pad for my new business ventures! My new websites www.ASREOS.com and www.REORESQ. com, (both created by Lindsay at www.CelebritySites.com) are fantastic and with all of the press generated by your program my business is off the charts! Thanks for helping me over the last 10 months and for always being personally available to answer my questions. You are true professionals."

– Frank Patrick

"When we signed up to work with Nick, Jack and his team we were expecting to be exposed to ideas on how to get more publicity. We never expected the 'red carpet' treatment we have received. To say that we are pleased with the experience we've had with you would be a mammoth understatement. Not only have you guys worked with us on how to improve the branding of our existing business you have used your expertise to help us launch a franchise that will take us to a completely different level.

The Ultimate Celebrity Branding Experience® has proved to be an investment that has and will literally change our business and our lives. As you know, my partner and I have participated in 'coaching groups' for years, in fact we run one for college planning guys, so we've seen just about everything in the 'we'll help you do... world'". We can testify that you guys are hands down the best in the business.

You guys are awesome, keep up the good work. I feel like we're family, and if you ever need anything, just let us know."

– Ron Caruthers

"Entering the final stage of the America's Premier Experts® program, I am in a great position to SHOUT about the outstanding nature of this program. I have been featured in national publications, interviewed by a top journalist, and will be appearing on TV in the very near future. Nick, Jack and the whole staff know their stuff when it comes to promotion of persons and businesses. Trust me-you need to be one of America's Premier Experts!®"

– James R. Parrish

"Nick & Jack do everything they say and then some. If you want a team to rev up your celebrity status, these are the folks to do it! They have more ideas than most people and best of all, they implement them."

– Dr. Gayle Carson

"If you are looking to promote your business and explode the growth then come see these guys that can help you do that."

– James Brown

"Celebrities are watched, stalked, worshiped and more than anything else, listened to! Think of the power a celebrity has — people want to know what they eat, what they wear, and where they go, they are the ultimate sales vehicle. People will wear what they wear, eat what they eat, and say what they say. When I first heard of the Ultimate Celebrity Branding Experience® I was more than skeptical. I quickly realized that Nick and Jack are on to something huge. If you are a celebrity in your field you are set for life, and the Ultimate Celebrity Branding Experience® is the short cut to being the celebrity you want to be."

– Tyrell Gray

"What you'll learn here I don't think you're going to get anywhere else. It's direct experience and it's the "how to" and you can take it back and immediately implement it and that's what you need to know how to do. Thank you Nick, Jack and Lindsay."

– Madeline Ross

"The whole experience from A-Z, is well thought out, well planned, we surround ourselves with great, successful, like-minded entrepreneurs. What a great place to be to meet people, network and get some million-dollar ideas. Thanks a lot to America's PremierExperts® hosts, Nick and Jack.

– Richard Seppala

"The Ultimate Celebrity Branding Experience® has added that extra edge of credibility that was needed to take my business to the next level. I am confident that it's helped seal my position as The national expert on sales for the Seniors Housing & Health Care industry."

– Traci Bild

"The Ultimate Celebrity Branding Experience® has been a first class experience that will continue to pay us dividends now and into the future of our business, Cater Galante Orthodontics. The team at the Celebrity Branding Agency truly care deeply about their clients and their clients' successes. Besides the definite benefit of growing your business, the relationships that you will develop with the other "experts" in your group will forge lifelong friendships and even business opportunities that are priceless. The investment in your "celebrity experience" is just that, an investment in yourself, your business and your future."

**– Dr. Donna Galante
and Dr. Paul Cater**

"There is nothing better than Celebrity Branding® and America's PremierExperts® to gain instant credibility as an expert in your field, go from a local expert to a national expert. This is hands down one of the best experiences to grow your business and Nick and the team at the Celebrity Branding® Agency deliver on every promise they make...and then some!

– Jennifer Myers

"The Ultimate Celebrity Branding Experience® has helped my business by teaching me how to be a celebrity in my own niche. I am able to gain exposure to a new population that didn't know who I was 12 months ago. The media exposure and credibility I have gained from this program is not only helping me now, but will help for the future as well with everything that I do in my niche."

– Jayson Hunter RD, CSCS

"I decided to sign up for the Ultimate Celebrity Branding Experience® in the fall of 2008 at the Info Summit. From that time Nick has truly been a great help. The first experience was just as they explained it would be...(Red carpet event). I have been able to use the publicity on my website, social networking pages and other media outlets.

Nick has done a great job and I think him and Jack for their efforts to help me, my partners and our company become the Celebrity we have needed to bump us to the next level."

– Brad Hess

"I didn't now what to expect when I decided to proceed with this venture and pleasantly surprised by everything the organization was phenomenal. Very professional, very courteous, very friendly made you feel as though you are the expert in the field that you do even though you may not feel that you are, and the confidence that they build, I'm ready to go conquer the world. So thanks guys, it was great and I can't wait to keep proceeding with this."

– Dr. Vesna Sutter

"Right after we did our T.V. Show in L.A., Fox 40 News in Sacramento called us two days later, came in to our office and did a live interview. So The [Ultimate] Celebrity Branding Experience is amazing, it's great for your business...I highly recommend it!"

– Donna Galante

Nick, You have assembled an impressive team, everyone I have dealt with thus far has shown a high degree of professionalism. I look forward to continuing to work with you and your company

– Marcus Holliman

"Look at US...we're freakin' rock stars!! Thanks ...Nick you have an incredible team!"

– David and Melina Montelongo

"A big thanks to DNAgency for all they have done to catapult me into being America's Premiere Cosmetic and Sedation Dentist. The masterminds and training are the biggest secrets to the success! SCHU BABY SCHU"

– Scott Schumann

As always, your team has produced a video segment that I will use repeatedly to establish my self as a celebrity expert. I'm proud to add this to the catalog of work you've done as my celebrity business agent.

– Chuck Boyce

"I'm simply blown away by the integrity, responsiveness, personal attention and RESULTS from Nick Nanton and his team at the Celebrity Branding Agency. They helped my business achieve MAJOR visibility all over the world, but especially here in the United States, which forms the bedrock of my client list.

"And not only is having my information (written beautifully by his team) "out there", but the search engine optimization factor for having my business be so authoritatively covered by major media outlets has ensured a solid foundation for any other web presence work my team and I undertake.

"In short, I can't recommend working with their team more highly! (And don't be put off by Nick's fast-talking style — the dude is the real deal, and simple extremely enthusiastic about what he does. Rightly so.)"

– Nate Hagerty

Excellent-great. Celebrity Branding is awesome. Thanks for being so responsive. I am getting so excited!

– Aynn Daniels

Nick, I now have a link to the video of my appearance on your TV show on my marketing mailers. I'm loving it AND, my income has tripled! WooHoo! Thank you, because of you and your team, and your TV show that I was on...I can put myself into a much better place and hit up the higher priced homes because...I am the expert!

– Loretta Washburn

Hi Nick, Just wanted to say thanks for the encouraging emails and really useful tips and observations that you send out. I rarely respond, but wanted you to know that I do read your emails and have learned a lot. Thanks! Have a great day.

– Silvia Nina

Nick, Jack and Lindsay, out of all the years I've been in business, I've NEVER seen ANYONE offer the media, marketing and PR triple threat that you guys do. You guys are MASTERS! Thanks for all you've done and continue you to do for me to help me build my business!"

– Ted Thomas

When I met Nick and Jack, my business was called Total Census Solutions, which was relevant to the niche I first started in (Senior Housing), but to the rest of the world it was confusing and very forgettable. Just by reviewing my Bio, before we even had much time to speak, Nick and Jack shot back a bunch of ideas about how my business was really centered around getting people the maximum ROI in their advertising, and spun out The ROI Guy brand for me. In the past 2 years since they helped me reinvent my brand, my business has taken off! Now everywhere I go, people call me the ROI Guy, which is fun, however, the most important thing is they also know where to call when they need solutions for tracking their marketing campaigns and getting the greatest ROI! Oh yeah, and they also like to have a bit of fun too!

– Richard Seppala

"Hi this is Kimberlee Frank "The Real Estate Junkie" and I am writing to let you know how joining America's PremierExperts® made a difference in my life. First off, I have shared the stage with a lot of people. However, it was always me having to impress my audience. Now, thanks to America›s PremierExperts®, I have a long list of credentials that allows me to get on any stage. The media coverage was out of this world. The friendship with Jack, Nick, and Lindsay is something that can not be replaced, we will always be connected. I have written many courses and wanted to write a book but never seemed to find time. With the help of America's PremierExperts®, they made it happen and not in years but everything was done in just 12 months. I just wanted to say "Thanks". I couldn›t have gotten this type of media coverage, book, and articles without your help. I would recommend this experience to anyone who is seriously looking to build their creditability fast!

– Kimberlee Frank

"I mentioned to you while we were in Hollywood that the day before I came, I got a call from a producer who found me through a press release and my participation in America's PremierExperts®. I had a phone interview and received an email inviting me out for an all expenses paid shoot for a TV show, where they want me to talk all about my business and what I do. I just wanted you to know how much I enjoy working with you all and think what you are doing is terrific. The fact is, what you guys are doing works. There is absolutely no way they would have found me, nor would I have this interview without you guys. The great thing is I can use whatever they produce in my arsenal now and hopefully get more interviews. So, again, thank you for everything—it works!!!"

– Jennifer Myers

"Nick & Jack do everything they say and then some. If you want a team to rev up your celebrity status, these are the folks to do it! They have more ideas than most people and best of all, they implement them.

– Dr. Gayle Carson

Nick, We were interviewed live today by Fox 40 News in Sacramento. They interviewed us in our office in Rocklin Ca and it was live at around 8:50 am PST. They will show the piece again at during the 10 pm News program.

We were also featured on the front page of our local newspaper, The Placer Herald. Paul's picture was on the front page and my photo (working on a patient) on the third page. We had a front page article about us and our practice!

This would not have happened without you and Jack and Lindsay and the entire team at Celebrity Branding!

Thanks so much!

– Donna Galante & Paul Cater

"I chose Dicks Nanton Agency because they get it. A lot of people provide marketing and PR but I was impressed with their ability to understand what drives a customer to do business with you. That's pretty rare. I really felt that I needed a fresh vision in my business to help us pull off the extraordinary for our clients.

I'm looking to Dicks Nanton Agency to provide fresh insight into Florida Leisure Vacation Homes and to help me take it to the next level,"

– Nigel Worrall

"I was looking for highly skilled, professional, high tech/ human touch resources to grow our distinctive exercise and health franchise. I needed people with great energy, who are very successful, because they use the resources they offer their clients...Dicks Nanton Agency has done that and has demonstrated wisdom and innovation in an ever-changing and demanding global market. As consultants, I needed someone 'to act as if' SuperSlow Zone is their company- to have the capacity and stamina to deliver on their promises for us, the franchisor, and all of the franchisees, JW Dicks, Nick Nanton and the Dicks Nanton Agency fit that bill. In addition to the aforementioned, for leverage and wise-economy, Dicks Nanton is '3-in-1': legal, marketing and strategic development... it is said that three heads are better than one... and they have proven this over and over."

– Madeline Ross

When we first met Nick and Jack, we were floundering a little with our training business...we had all of the pieces, but didn't have a cohesive vision or strategy of where it could take us. Since working with them, we have put more systems into our office, we are looking at the marketing (and the results of that marketing!) in a whole new light, our website actually looks like a professional did it, AND we have an awesome vision for our company that will allow us to retire in just a few short years. Sometimes we get so busy in the day to day "stuff" of our businesses that we forget to stop and look AT our businesses, The Dicks + Nanton Agency has afforded us an impartial outsiders' view of our own business and the potential that it has.

– Andy Tolbert

I want to thank Nick and Jack for helping me make my dreams a reality. I came to them seeking advice for growing my business. Other people in the past have told me that my ideas and dreams for my business were unattainable. Jack and Nick teamed up with me to brand myself and have opened doors that, in the past, were closed. They have opened my mind to see all of the different ways to make my business successful and to take it to the next level. Thanks to them, today, I am in a position to achieve my business goals and am creating financial freedom for my family and my business partners.

– Ronel Jumpp

Jack & Nick have brought about more expansion in our business in the past three months than we thought possible. They got us to see the big picture while explaining everything along the way. Jack and Nick took the time to understand our business goals and tailored their approach to us. We wouldn't trust our company with anyone else!

– Jon Ruhff & Yeosh Bendayan

"You are the best....thank you for an amazing experience! We are so honored to be a part of what you are doing!"

– Missy McCullough

"Great experience with these guys. A total class act."

– Peter D'Arruda

I was just at the National Speakers Association Convention and met Nick Nanton. He has a professional operation for sure but what most impressed me most was what happened after that day we met; He had listened closely to my business plan and history and when I got off my plane, home in San Francisco, I saw he had emailed me. He detailed a brilliantly thought out title series for my book series and keynote series. It was creative. It was perfect. I was impressed. Nick Nanton is a first class act and the real deal.

– Massari

"JW Dicks and Nick Nanton, in their book, reveal one of the true business secrets that pratically all entrepreneurs miss... which is to brand yourself. At Glazer-Kennedy Insider's Circle (dankennedy.com) we have been teaching for years that you want to run a celebrity driven business and what's more important is to make yourself the celebrity! In "CELEBRITY BRANDING YOU(tm)" they do a superb job of walking you through this invaluable process from A-Z. This is a must read for every business owner and entrepreneur.

– Bill Glazer,
President Glazer-Kennedy Insider's Circle™

Like any vehicle, it will run smoothly if and only if 1) the right fuel is used, 2) you make it a priority to maintain it, 3) and you have a great mechanic! As a business owner, having your team in place is critical to success. I was happy with my original website; giving birth to it was a process. But after a while, as it grows so do your needs. You change or your brand changes. It was not a coincidence that I met Lindsay Dicks from Celebrity Sites; it was time...call it synchronicity at work. I had been rethinking my website and needed to delegate more of what I was choosing not to do regarding social media and web maintenance. I have never been so impressed by their professionalism, dedication or follow-through. They are there at a moments notice to work through my questions, my ideas or concerns. I give them straight A pluses. They have me for LIFE.

— **Sallie Felton,**
Life Coach/Transition Specialist,
International Talk Radio Host
#1 Best Selling Author, IF I'M
SO SMART, WHY CAN'T I GET
RID OF THIS CLUTTER?

"It's always scary changing your website even when you know you need an update. Lots of times you feel like you are on an island and the people developing your website could care less if they respond to your concerns or not. Not only did Lindsay and her staff stay in constant contact with me through the entire process, they responded immediately to each question, and improved on my own ideas for the site. They thought of things that I would have never considered and have also taken my haphazard social media postings and formed a consistent strategy that is sure to blow the doors off anything I have done before. I feel like I have gotten many times over my money's worth already. Thanks Lindsay and team!"

— **Dr. Chris Griffin,**
Ripley, MS,
The Capacity Academy

Want to hear *Ka-ching again?* Well, if your website's dead, not making money and you don't how to fix it – good news, there's an answer.

Call Lindsay Dicks and her staff at CelebritySites!

They simply know the 'stuff' you and I don't – important 'stuff' that actually works, creating a website that gets the phone to ring… and online sales to grow!

So, humble yourself, *just a little*, like we did, and let these guys replace or revitalize your old *billboard* type website with a dynamic marketing platform one that's designed to 'pull' in sales in a completely different way.

It's more than a website – it's a complete, pedal to the metal, marketing strategy! And, it's more than worth the little 'shot' to the ego.

One last thing…forget generalities – check this out! Our site was basically 'dead in the water' until Lindsay and her gang turned it into an interest grabbing, marketing platform.

NOW, we enjoy **1st page ranking** on, not one, but THREE of our main keywords. Our website went from an online brochure to a virtual *"living, breathing, marketing machine!"*

Yeah, we like the folks at CelebritySites.com a lot. YOU will too!

– Daniel J. Liebrecht,
Clean Guru LLC

"I just got off the phone with a reporter for SmartMoney.com for an article about foreclosures that's going to run on AOL.com in about 2 weeks! She found me by searching on Google and found the press release you did that announced me as a new "expert" for AgentDirectNews.com. Then she went to my website and liked what she saw so she called me up! Imagine, being quoted in an AOL Real Estate story…you can't BUY that kind of exposure at any price! I knew I was making the right choice to work with you guys and now that has been confirmed ten fold! Thanks for all of your help!"

– Andy Tolbert

"The online world is a great place to make money and gain notoriety but it can be a tremendous waste of resources if you don't have the right team working with you. When my previous consulting company was charging me outrageous prices and failing to deliver time and time again, I turned to Celebrity Sites®. Since then my online campaigns have turned around 180 degrees! Its great having Celebrity Sites® on my team, helping me grow my business and my profits. Don't wait until its too late, call them today. Trust me, you can't afford to wait!"

– Chris Hurn,
President and CEO, Mercantile
Capital Corporation®

Honestly, you guys are the best. I appreciate all that you do and will do for your clients. You guys really go one step and beyond and I will recommend you to everyone.

– Richard Seppala,
The ROI Guy

Just wanted to take a minute to thank Celebrity Sites. Making that first impression of what our business is about is very important.

Celebrity Sites has done more in just a couple of months than we did in the last 6 years which was nothing because we tried different things but were just were not on track. You knew where to start and how to get there in lighting speed. You guys not only listened to our ideas but gave some great ideas. Whenever we needed to talk to you, you were right there, by email or phone – you name it, you responded. We are so excited every day to see Larry's Big Idea take shape. The website is second to none thanks to Lindsay and is improving weekly. The ideas that Jack and Nick come up with at each meeting are awesome.

If anyone out there is considering launching their business to just the next level forget it. Get in the elevator with Celebrity Sites and they will take you to the top floor (Penthouse). Stay tuned for more!

– Kimberlee Frank

Celebrity Sites® is awesome! They are on top of things all the time and keep you out in front of your competition. Thanks again and again!

– Larry Frank
(aka Mr. Prepared)

CNBC Contacted me because of Celebrity Sites®!

I just wanted to take a moment to say WOW! My last website took many years and many versions to never quite get what I wanted. In less than 30 days you guys designed and built a brand new website that I love and now, not even 60 days since it's been live, I'm starting to get calls from television producers! Just last week I got a call from CNBC because they were searching for financial experts to feature on a new show they are launching and they found me thanks to my new website. This is incredible, thanks so much for the great experience. Anyone who isn't taking advantage of your unique expertise of Celebrity Branding business people online is missing the boat in many ways!

– Brian Fricke,
Owner, President

Thanks Celebrity Sites®! With your help we just got picked up on a worldwide site for our music buffet option. They even put it on the front page of their site as a "breakthrough"! Our site, art and design looks fantastic. Well done! We couldn't do it without you!"

– Yeosh and Jon,
Push Button Productions

Wow, you really know what you are doing & I am impressed! CelebritySites took my dead website & literally brought it to life! I never realized what I was missing until my site was completely revamped! Thank you, thank you, thank you!

– Traci Bild

"Thanks for everything! We're crushing last year's numbers, already. Thanks for helping us spread the word!"

– Neill Foshee,
Senior Equity Advisor,
Hidden Wealth System

"I love working with Nick and his team. They can absolutely help you get to the next level. Nick does everything he promises and then some!"

– Jack Canfield,
Best-Selling Author of more than
500 million books. Co-Creator
of "Chicken Soup for the Soul"
series

CPSIA information can be obtained at www.ICGtesting.com
Printed in the USA
BVOW07*1140210814

363481BV00001B/1/P